Acadia National Park Travel Guide 2024

Discover the Natural Beauty, Outdoor Activities, and Hidden Gems: Top Attractions, Hotels, and Restaurants

Lovelyn Hill

Table of Contents

Introduction

Acadia National Park, a realm of rugged coastal beauty and untamed wilderness, beckons you to immerse yourself in its awe-inspiring landscapes and rich tapestry of experiences. As you stand on the precipice of this natural wonder, prepare to embark on a journey that transcends the ordinary—a journey through the heart of Acadia.

Here, where the Atlantic Ocean cradles the rocky shores of Maine, nature unfolds in a spectacular display of granite peaks, verdant forests, and the timeless ebb and flow of tides. Acadia National Park, established in 1919, is not merely a destination; it's a sanctuary where the soul connects with the wild.

In the pages of this guide, I unveil the secrets of Acadia, guiding you through a landscape sculpted by ancient forces and infused with a spirit that echoes through the rustling leaves, the crashing waves, and the calls of the soaring seabirds. My purpose is to be your compass in this realm of natural marvels, revealing the hidden gems, storied trails, and the pulse of life that beats beneath the granite peaks.

As the sun graces the mountaintops with its first light, Cadillac Mountain awakens, a sentinel overseeing the birth of a new day. The air is crisp, infused with the scent of pine and the promise of adventure. This guide is your key to unlocking the treasures concealed within Acadia's embrace, a roadmap to the vibrant landscapes and timeless wonders that have captivated explorers for generations.

The heart of Acadia beats in rhythm with the pounding waves along Thunder Hole, a natural amphitheater where the Atlantic showcases its power. Wander through the enchanting carriage roads, conceived by the vision of John D. Rockefeller Jr., or meander along the rugged coastline, where cliffs meet the sea in a dramatic ballet of nature's design. Acadia isn't just a place; it's a living, breathing testament to the beauty of the world we inhabit.

Your journey through Acadia extends beyond the well-worn paths to the hidden nooks and crannies, where the true essence of the park lies. Uncover secret coves, explore forgotten ruins, and witness the sunset from secluded vantage points—the undiscovered chapters of Acadia that await your curious spirit.

Dining in Acadia isn't just a culinary adventure; it's a celebration of local flavors and traditions. From seaside lobster shacks to fine dining establishments with panoramic ocean views, savor the tastes of the region and let your palate become part of the park's rich narrative.

The lodgings offered within Acadia are not mere places to rest your head; they are sanctuaries that complement the natural wonders outside your window. Whether you choose the opulence of luxury hotels, the comfort of mid-range establishments, or the charm of budget-friendly options, each accommodation is a gateway to your Acadia experience.

Acadia National Park isn't just a destination; it's an invitation to step into a world where nature reigns supreme, where every trail leads to a discovery, and every sunset paints a new masterpiece. This guide is your passport to the extraordinary, offering insights, recommendations, and a curated roadmap to help you create your unforgettable narrative within the embrace of Acadia. So, let the journey begin, and may your adventure in Acadia be nothing short of extraordinary.

Nestled along the rugged Atlantic coastline of Maine, Acadia National Park stands as a testament to the raw beauty and untamed wilderness that defines the northeastern United States. As you contemplate the decision to embark on a journey to this captivating destination, the question arises: Why visit Acadia National Park?

Why Visit Acadia National Park

An Array of Natural Diversity

Acadia National Park, spanning 49,000 acres, boasts a remarkably diverse landscape that seamlessly intertwines mountains, forests, lakes, and an intricate coastline. Cadillac Mountain, the highest point on the East Coast, offers panoramic views of a terrain that reflects the eons of geological forces at play. The juxtaposition of granite peaks against the expanse of the Atlantic Ocean creates a visual masterpiece that lures nature enthusiasts, hikers, and adventure seekers from around the globe.

Unique Coastal Splendor

Unlike any other national park, Acadia's coastline is a mesmerizing fusion of rugged cliffs, tidal pools, and serene coves. Thunder Hole, where the Atlantic crashes against the granite shoreline, provides a symphony of nature's power. Jordan Pond, with its crystal-clear waters reflecting the surrounding mountains, serves as a serene oasis. The iconic Bass Harbor Head Lighthouse stands as a sentinel, guiding ships through the craggy shores and marking a chapter in maritime history.

Immersive Outdoor Experiences

Acadia National Park is a playground for outdoor enthusiasts, offering an array of activities for all levels of adventurers. Over 120 miles of hiking trails weave through forests and ascend to panoramic vistas. The Carriage Roads, a network of meticulously designed paths by philanthropist John D. Rockefeller Jr., wind through valleys and around lakes, perfect for biking and strolls. Whether scaling the challenging Precipice Trail or indulging in a tranquil lakeside picnic, Acadia provides a canvas for a myriad of outdoor pursuits.

Seasonal Transformations

One of Acadia's charms lies in its ever-changing face with each passing season. Spring unveils a carpet of wildflowers, and fall bathes the landscape in hues of red and gold. Winter, though quieter, transforms the park into a snowy wonderland, inviting cross-country skiers and snowshoers to explore its trails. Summer, with warm temperatures and extended daylight, draws visitors seeking the quintessential outdoor experience.

Rich Cultural and Historical Significance

Beyond its natural wonders, Acadia carries a rich tapestry of cultural and historical significance. Native American tribes, including the Wabanaki people, have long considered this land sacred. The park's history is intertwined with the preservation efforts of individuals like George B. Dorr and John D. Rockefeller Jr., who played pivotal roles in establishing and shaping Acadia National Park into what it is today.

Sustainable Tourism and Preservation

Visiting Acadia National Park isn't merely an adventure; it's a commitment to the preservation of natural beauty. The park's sustainability initiatives, including Leave No Trace practices and conservation efforts, ensure that future generations can continue to marvel at its wonders. By treading lightly and respecting the delicate balance of ecosystems, visitors become stewards of this ecological haven.

What to Expect in this Guide

As you embark on your journey to explore the enchanting wonders of Acadia National Park, this guide is your compass, designed to transform your visit into an extraordinary adventure. Here's a glimpse of what you can expect within these pages:

Comprehensive Insights into Acadia's Rich Tapestry

Uncover the layers of Acadia's history, geography, and cultural significance. From the ancient stories embedded in its landscapes to the conservation efforts that have preserved its pristine beauty, this guide provides a holistic view of Acadia National Park.

Detailed Itinerary Suggestions

Navigate Acadia with confidence using our meticulously crafted itineraries. Whether you have a day or a week, we offer diverse suggestions for maximizing your time, ensuring you don't miss the must-see attractions and hidden gems that define the park.

Top Attractions Unveiled

Delve into detailed explorations of Acadia's top attractions, including Cadillac Mountain, Jordan Pond, Thunder Hole, and many more. Each section provides a comprehensive overview, allowing you to plan your visit with a clear understanding of the unique offerings of each destination.

Activities for Every Adventurer

Discover a multitude of activities catering to various interests and skill levels. Whether you're an avid hiker, a wildlife enthusiast, or simply seeking tranquility, our guide offers a diverse range of activities to suit every adventurer's taste.

Culinary and Dining Adventures

Embark on a culinary journey through Acadia's vibrant dining scene. From seafood shacks to upscale bistros, we guide you to the best dining experiences, ensuring your taste buds savor the flavors of the region.

Accommodations Tailored to Your Preferences

Choose the perfect sanctuary for your stay with our comprehensive recommendations for luxury hotels, mid-range accommodations, and budget-friendly options. Each suggestion is carefully curated to enhance your overall experience while providing comfort and convenience.

Hidden Gems and Off-the-Beaten-Path Discoveries

Unearth the secrets of Acadia with our insights into hidden gems and lesser-known trails. Venture beyond the well-trodden paths to encounter secluded coves, historic ruins, and picturesque spots that offer a more intimate connection with the park.

Practical Tips for a Seamless Adventure

Navigate Acadia with ease using our practical tips and advice. From packing essentials to safety guidelines and sustainable tourism practices, this guide equips you with the knowledge needed for a seamless and responsible exploration.

As your trusted companion, this guide aims to elevate your Acadia National Park experience, ensuring that every moment becomes a cherished memory. Whether you're a first-time visitor or a seasoned explorer, embark on this journey with the assurance that every page holds the key to unlocking the unparalleled beauty of Acadia.

Chapter 1

Getting to Know Acadia

Geography and Climate

As you stand on the threshold of Acadia National Park, the first chapter of your adventure unfolds in the rich tapestry of its geography and climate. Here, the landscape becomes a living canvas, painted with the vibrant hues of dense forests, granite peaks, and the undulating coastline of the Atlantic. It's a symphony of nature, each element playing its part in the masterpiece that is Acadia.

Geography

Acadia's heart lies primarily on Mount Desert Island, a rugged gem surrounded by the inky blue embrace of the Atlantic Ocean. Extending beyond its island boundaries, the park also encompasses the Schoodic Peninsula and Isle au Haut, ensuring that every corner is a new exploration waiting to happen.

The crowning jewel of Acadia is Cadillac Mountain, reaching an elevation of 1,530 feet. As the highest peak along the eastern seaboard, Cadillac Mountain promises panoramic vistas that redefine the concept of breathtaking. Picture yourself at its summit, the first place in the United States touched by the morning sun, and as you gaze upon the undulating landscape below, the magic of Acadia unfolds before your eyes.

The rugged terrain, shaped by ancient glaciers and softened by the hands of time, unveils a network of over 120 miles of hiking trails. These trails wind through lush forests, leading you to hidden valleys, serene lakes, and awe-inspiring viewpoints. Jordan Pond, nestled amidst rolling hills and bordered by the twin peaks known as the Bubbles, is a tranquil expanse that invites reflection and repose.

7

Climate

Acadia's climate, like its landscape, is a study in contrasts. Embrace the ebb and flow of the seasons, each bringing its magic to the park.

In the embrace of spring, witness the resurrection of nature as blossoms adorn the landscape, and migratory birds return to fill the air with their melodious songs. The moderate temperatures make this season perfect for exploring Acadia's diverse ecosystems without the summer crowds.

Summer unveils the park in all its glory, with warm days inviting exploration and cool evenings providing respite. The coastline comes alive with visitors seeking the solace of sandy beaches and the rhythmic lullaby of the ocean. Be prepared for a kaleidoscope of colors as the sun dips below the horizon, casting a warm glow over the granite peaks.

Fall transforms Acadia into a canvas of reds, oranges, and golds. The crisp air and the crunch of fallen leaves underfoot accompany you as you traverse the trails. Capture the park in its autumnal splendor, where every turn reveals a postcard-worthy scene.

Winter, though quieter, casts Acadia in a serene blanket of snow. The landscape transforms into a winter wonderland, offering a different perspective for those who seek solitude and the crisp beauty of snow-draped trees.

Flora and Fauna

As you traverse the diverse landscapes of Acadia National Park, a hidden world of flora and fauna unfurls before your eyes, weaving a delicate tapestry of life that is as enchanting as it is resilient. Acadia, with its varied ecosystems, plays host to a captivating array of plant and animal species, inviting you to explore the intricate dance of nature within its boundaries.

Flora

Acadia's flora is a study in adaptation, a testament to nature's ingenuity in the face of challenging terrains and ever-changing climates. Traverse the park's trails, and you'll encounter a kaleidoscope of plant life, each species finding its niche in this ecological haven.

The dense woodlands are home to a variety of conifers, such as spruce and fir, creating a fragrant canopy that shelters the forest floor. As you wander through the trails, notice the delicate blossoms of wildflowers carpeting the landscape in hues of white, yellow, and purple. From the elusive lady's slipper orchid to the vibrant fireweed, Acadia's flora offers a sensory feast that changes with the seasons.

The coastal regions, with their salty breezes and rocky shores, harbor resilient plant life that has adapted to withstand the harsh conditions. Sturdy shrubs like bayberry and rugosa a rose thrive, their leaves glistening with salt crystals, adding a touch of green to the rugged, windswept scenery.

Fauna

Acadia's diverse habitats support an impressive array of wildlife, creating a living, breathing ecosystem that adds depth to your journey. Keep your eyes peeled, and you might catch a glimpse of the park's resident fauna, each species playing a vital role in the delicate balance of nature.

White-tailed deer, their graceful forms moving through the forest understory, are a common sight. Red foxes, with their fiery coats, may

9

stealthily cross your path, while the elusive bobcat, a symbol of wilderness, remains a more mysterious presence.

Birdwatchers will find Acadia to be a haven, with over 330 recorded species. Peregrine falcons soar above the cliffs, their keen eyes searching for prey, while the haunting calls of loons echo across the park's lakes. During the migratory season, songbirds add a symphony of melodies to the air, creating a soundtrack for your exploration.

Historical Significance

As you delve into the heart of Acadia National Park, you are stepping onto the sacred ground with a rich tapestry of human history that echoes through the rustling leaves and craggy cliffs. Acadia's story is not just about landscapes and wildlife; it's a journey through time, tracing the footprints of indigenous peoples, visionaries, and conservationists who collectively shaped this extraordinary sanctuary.

Indigenous Heritage

Long before the park's establishment, the Wabanaki people, comprising the Penobscot, Passamaquoddy, Mi'kmaq, Maliseet, and Abenaki tribes, called this region home. Their deep connection to the land is woven into the very fabric of Acadia's landscape. As you tread upon its trails, imagine the Wabanaki people navigating these woods, harvesting from the bountiful forests, and forging a profound spiritual connection with the land.

George B. Dorr and the Founding of Acadia

The visionary George B. Dorr, often referred to as the "Father of Acadia," played a pivotal role in the park's establishment. Infatuated with the beauty of Mount Desert Island, Dorr dedicated decades of his life to preserving this natural wonder. His passion culminated in 1916 when he donated large portions of land to the federal government, laying the foundation for what would become Acadia National Park in 1919. Dorr's foresight ensured that future generations could revel in the splendor of Acadia's landscapes.

John D. Rockefeller Jr. and the Carriage Roads

Another influential figure in Acadia's history is John D. Rockefeller Jr. Inspired by a desire to experience the park without the intrusion of automobiles, Rockefeller funded and oversaw the construction of the Carriage Roads. Over 50 miles of these meticulously crafted paths wind through the park, providing a serene network for hikers, cyclists, and horseback riders to explore the wilderness with minimal impact on the environment.

The Civilian Conservation Corps (CCC) Legacy

During the Great Depression, the Civilian Conservation Corps left an indelible mark on Acadia. Young men, part of this New Deal program, worked tirelessly to build trails, construct bridges, and develop the park's infrastructure. Their legacy lives on in the network of paths and structures that facilitate your exploration of Acadia's diverse terrains.

Bass Harbor Head Lighthouse

Nestled on the southwestern tip of Mount Desert Island, the Bass Harbor Head Lighthouse stands as both a functional beacon for mariners and a historic landmark. Built in 1858, the lighthouse has witnessed the passage of time, guiding ships through treacherous waters and serving as a symbol of maritime heritage.

War Years and Naval Intelligence Station

During World War II, the U.S. Navy established a naval intelligence station on Mount Desert Island, utilizing the park's commanding views for strategic purposes. The remnants of this wartime activity add a layer of historical intrigue to the landscape.

As you explore Acadia, let the echoes of history guide your journey. Every trail, every landmark, and every rustling leaf tells a story of resilience, vision, and a deep-seated commitment to preserving the natural wonders that define this iconic national park. Acadia's historical significance isn't just a chapter in a book; it's an immersive experience that allows you to walk in the footsteps of those who recognized the extraordinary value of this land and sought to protect it for generations to come.

Chapter 2

Planning Your Trip

When to Visit

As you embark on the journey to uncover the natural wonders of Acadia National Park, strategic planning is your key to unlocking the optimal experience. Choosing the right time to visit is akin to orchestrating a symphony, harmonizing with the seasonal nuances that define this breathtaking destination.

Spring: A Blossoming Canvas (Late April to Early June)

In the tender embrace of spring, Acadia transforms into a vibrant canvas adorned with a tapestry of wildflowers and awakening wildlife. Late April to early June marks the onset of this enchanting season, where the landscape emerges from winter's slumber. The air is crisp, infused with the fragrance of blooming flora, and the trails come alive with a burst of color. If you cherish the idea of hiking amidst nature's reawakening, spring is your golden window.

Summer: Peak Splendor (Late June to Early September)

For the quintessential Acadia experience, summer unfolds as the peak season. From late June to early September, the park embraces a symphony of activities under the warm embrace of the sun. Days are long, allowing you to make the most of your exploration. Whether hiking to the summit of Cadillac Mountain, biking along carriage roads, or basking on the sandy shores, summer presents Acadia in its full splendor. However, do anticipate larger crowds during this time, and plan accordingly to secure accommodations and popular tour reservations.

Fall: Nature's Canvas of Fire (Late September to Early November)

As the sun descends lower on the horizon, Acadia transitions into a captivating display of autumnal hues. Late September to early November paints the landscape with fiery reds, oranges, and golden yellows. Fall is a photographer's delight, with the reflection of changing leaves on the serene waters of Jordan Pond and the juxtaposition against the rugged coastline. The crisp air invites hikers to traverse the trails adorned in a kaleidoscope of colors, making fall a sought-after season for those seeking a more serene and visually stunning experience.

Winter: A Tranquil Wonderland (Late November to Early April)

While winter bestows a hushed tranquility upon Acadia, it unveils a different facet of its beauty. Late November to early April welcomes a snow-covered wonderland, inviting winter enthusiasts to explore cross-country skiing and snowshoeing trails. The park's serene ambiance during winter provides a unique opportunity for solitude and reflection. Keep in mind that some facilities and roads may be closed, but the reward is the chance to witness Acadia in its serene, snow-draped elegance.

Factors to Consider

In deciding when to visit, consider your preferred activities and tolerance for crowds. Each season offers a distinct flavor, allowing you to tailor your trip to your preferences. If you prioritize solitude and a winter wonderland, venture during the colder months. For a balance of activities and optimal weather, summer might be the ideal choice. Spring and fall provide a compromise, offering a mix of blooming beauty or vibrant foliage with fewer visitors.

As you delve into the intricacies of planning your Acadia adventure, remember that each season unveils a unique charm. Whether it's the burgeoning life of spring, the vibrant energy of summer, the captivating hues of fall, or the tranquil serenity of winter, Acadia awaits you with open arms, ready to weave its magic into your unforgettable journey.

Travel Essentials

Clothing and Gear

In the dynamic microclimates of Acadia, where mountainous terrain meets the ocean breeze, versatile clothing is paramount. Layering is your ally, ensuring adaptability to temperature fluctuations. A sturdy pair of hiking boots provide traction on uneven trails, and don't forget a reliable waterproof jacket—after all, Acadia's weather can be as diverse as its landscapes.

Navigation Tools

While Acadia's trails are well-marked, having a map and compass as backup ensures you stay on course. Alternatively, consider a GPS device or a reliable hiking app on your smartphone to enhance your navigation prowess, especially if you plan to explore the park's extensive network of trails.

Daypack Essentials

A well-packed daypack is your mobile command center. Load it with essentials such as water, snacks, a first aid kit, sunscreen, insect repellent, and a headlamp. This ensures you're ready for the unexpected and can comfortably explore Acadia's wonders without interruptions.

Binoculars and Camera

Acadia is a haven for birdwatchers and photography enthusiasts. Binoculars enhance your birding experience, while a camera captures the ephemeral beauty of the landscapes. Whether you're aiming for the sunrise atop Cadillac Mountain or the intricate details of wildflowers, these tools become your window into Acadia's soul.

National Park Pass

To traverse the gates of Acadia, a National Park Pass is your golden ticket. Available for purchase online or at park entrances, this pass provides access to the park and supports conservation efforts. Opt for the annual pass if you plan to explore multiple national parks during your travels.

Camping Gear

For those seeking a more immersive experience, Acadia offers various campsites. If camping is on your agenda, ensure your gear includes a reliable tent, sleeping bag, and camp stove. Familiarize yourself with the park's camping regulations and secure any necessary permits in advance.

Personal Identification and Documentation

While exploring Acadia, having identification and relevant documentation is essential. Keep your driver's license, passport, and any reservation confirmations handy. Additionally, if you plan to partake in ranger-led programs or activities, consider having your park map and program schedule readily accessible.

Weather-Appropriate Accessories

Acadia's weather is as diverse as its landscapes. Depending on the season, pack weather-appropriate accessories such as a sun hat, gloves, or even snowshoes if venturing during the winter months. Be prepared for sudden changes in weather, and always check the forecast before setting out.

Snacks and Hydration

Exploration requires energy. Pack a selection of energizing snacks, ensuring a balance of proteins and carbohydrates. Staying hydrated is equally crucial, so carry a refillable water bottle. Acadia's trails may lead you to breathtaking vistas, but they also demand replenishment to keep you fueled for the next adventure.

Leave No Trace Ethics

Beyond physical items, carry a sense of responsibility. Familiarize yourself with Leave No Trace principles, advocating for the preservation of Acadia's pristine beauty. Dispose of waste responsibly, stay on designated trails, and respect the natural environment to ensure future generations can enjoy the park's wonders.

Armed with these travel essentials, you're poised for an immersive and enjoyable exploration of Acadia National Park. Whether scaling peaks, meandering along coastal trails, or simply soaking in the cultural richness, these tools are the foundation for an unforgettable adventure in this coastal haven.

Entry Requirements

Entrance Fees and Passes

To access Acadia National Park, you'll need to pay an entrance fee or possess a valid pass. The entrance fees contribute to the park's conservation and maintenance efforts. Consider purchasing the Annual Pass if you plan to explore multiple national parks throughout the year, providing a cost-effective option for avid adventurers.

Pass Options

Acadia offers various pass options, each tailored to different visitor needs. The Seven-Day Entrance Pass is ideal for a shorter stay, while the Annual Pass grants year-round access to Acadia and other national parks. Additionally, specialized passes, such as the Senior Pass or Access Pass, provide discounted or free entry for qualifying individuals.

Online Purchase and Digital Passes

Streamline your entry process by purchasing your pass online before arriving at the park. Digital passes can be stored on your smartphone, offering a convenient and environmentally friendly option. Ensure that your pass is easily accessible, either in printed or digital form, as park rangers may request it upon entry.

Park Operating Hours and Seasons

Acadia's operating hours and seasons can impact your visit. Be aware of the park's opening and closing times, as well as any seasonal closures or restrictions. Plan your activities accordingly, considering the unique experiences each season brings, from blooming wildflowers in spring to snow-covered landscapes in winter.

Shuttle Service and Transportation

During peak seasons, Acadia offers a shuttle service to mitigate traffic and reduce environmental impact. Familiarize yourself with the shuttle routes and schedules, as it provides a convenient and eco-friendly way to access key park destinations. Additionally, consider carpooling or utilizing alternative transportation options to minimize congestion.

Backcountry Permits

For those venturing into Acadia's backcountry for camping or extended hikes, backcountry permits may be required. Research specific trail regulations and obtain the necessary permits in advance to ensure compliance with park regulations and facilitate a safe wilderness experience.

Ranger-Led Programs and Activities

Enhance your Acadia experience by participating in ranger-led programs and activities. Some programs may require reservations or have limited availability. Plan ahead by checking the park's schedule and booking in advance to secure your spot in these educational and immersive experiences.

Wildlife Safety and Regulations

Acadia is home to diverse wildlife, and respecting their habitat is crucial. Familiarize yourself with wildlife safety guidelines and park regulations. Maintain a safe distance, refrain from feeding animals, and follow Leave No Trace principles to ensure the preservation of the park's ecological balance.

Stay Informed and Flexible

Lastly, stay informed and flexible. Weather conditions, trail closures, or unforeseen circumstances may impact your plans. Check for updates on the park's official website, follow social media channels for real-time information, and be adaptable to changes to make the most of your Acadia adventure.

Acadia National Park Travel Guide 2024

Chapter 3

Top Attractions

Cadillac Mountain

Nestled within the heart of Acadia National Park, Cadillac Mountain stands as the crowning jewel, offering a panoramic vista that unfolds with unparalleled beauty. As the tallest peak along the Atlantic seaboard, Cadillac Mountain beckons adventurers to its summit, promising a breathtaking experience that transcends the ordinary.

Location

Situated on Mount Desert Island, Cadillac Mountain graces the eastern side of Acadia National Park. Rising to an elevation of 1,530 feet (466 meters), it holds the distinction of being the highest point on the United States East Coast.

How to Get There

Reaching the summit of Cadillac Mountain is a journey that can be tailored to your preferences. A winding road, the Cadillac Summit Road, offers a picturesque drive to the top. Alternatively, for the more adventurous souls, several hiking trails, such as the Cadillac South Ridge Trail, provide an invigorating ascent.

What to Expect

As you ascend Cadillac Mountain, a world of wonders unfolds before your eyes. The summit provides a 360-degree panorama, offering sweeping views of the Atlantic Ocean, neighboring islands, and the intricate landscapes of Acadia National Park. What sets Cadillac Mountain apart is its claim to fame as the first place in the United States to witness the sunrise from October 7 through March 6, making it a coveted destination for early risers seeking a celestial spectacle.

Things to Do

- Sunrise and Sunset Viewing: Cadillac Mountain is renowned for its breathtaking sunrise and sunset views. Arrive early to witness the dawn's first light or venture up in the evening to witness the sun bidding adieu in a blaze of colors.
- Stargazing: In the evening, the summit becomes a prime location for stargazing. The absence of city lights allows for a clear view of the night sky, offering a celestial spectacle that is both humbling and awe-inspiring.
- Hiking Trails: For those who prefer to earn their views, explore the various hiking trails leading to Cadillac Mountain. The South Ridge Trail, starting from the Tarn parking area, offers a challenging yet rewarding ascent.
- Photography: Capture the beauty of Acadia from a vantage point that promises unparalleled photo opportunities. The ever-changing play of light and shadow over the landscape creates a canvas that beckons photographers to frame its beauty.

Jordan Pond

Enveloped in tranquility and surrounded by the lush embrace of Acadia's landscapes, Jordan Pond stands as a testament to the park's pristine beauty. This idyllic glacial pond, nestled between the Penobscot and Sargent Mountains, is a haven for those seeking serenity and natural splendor.

Location

Located in the central part of Mount Desert Island, Jordan Pond is easily accessible and serves as a serene focal point within Acadia National Park.

How to Get There

To access Jordan Pond, follow the Park Loop Road, and signs will guide you to the Jordan Pond House, the starting point for your exploration. The Pond Loop Trail, encircling the water, provides an easy and picturesque stroll.

What to Expect

Jordan Pond's allure lies in its crystal-clear waters, reflecting the surrounding mountains and forests. The iconic North and South Bubbles, two rounded mountains, enhance the pond's beauty, creating a captivating backdrop. The peaceful ambiance and well-maintained paths make it an ideal destination for visitors of all ages.

Things to Do

- Afternoon Tea at Jordan Pond House: Indulge in a cherished tradition by partaking in afternoon tea at the historic Jordan Pond House. Surrounded by manicured lawns and overlooking the pond, this experience blends culinary delights with breathtaking views.
- Pond Loop Trail: Embark on the Pond Loop Trail, a 3.3-mile circuit around Jordan Pond. The trail offers a leisurely and family-friendly hike, presenting opportunities for birdwatching and taking in the scenery.
- Canoeing and Kayaking: During the warmer months, explore the tranquil waters of Jordan Pond by renting a canoe or kayak. Paddle at your own pace, immersing yourself in the serenity of this glacial oasis.
- Wildlife Observation: Jordan Pond is a haven for wildlife enthusiasts. Keep an eye out for resident beavers, dragonflies skimming the water's surface, and the diverse bird species that call this area home.

Thunder Hole

In the theater of Acadia's rugged coastline, Thunder Hole emerges as a natural marvel—a symphony of crashing waves, booming echoes, and the raw power of the Atlantic Ocean. This captivating site along Park Loop Road promises an immersive experience, where nature's forces converge to create an awe-inspiring spectacle.

Location

Thunder Hole is strategically positioned along the Ocean Path, found on the eastern side of Mount Desert Island in Acadia National Park. This site, with its unique geological formations, amplifies the auditory and visual drama of the ocean's power.

How to Get There

Accessible via the Park Loop Road, Thunder Hole is a prominent stop along this scenic route. Visitors can park at designated areas and follow the short trail leading to the observation area, ensuring a front-row seat to nature's orchestration.

What to Expect

True to its name, Thunder Hole is renowned for the resounding thunderous boom created when waves collide with an underwater cavern. The site's granite formations intensify the sound, resulting in a reverberating echo that resonates through the air. During high tide, especially under stormy conditions, the waves can reach astonishing heights, creating a mesmerizing display of nature's raw power.

Things to Do

- Witness the Spectacle: Position yourself at the observation area and witness the mesmerizing spectacle as waves crash against the rocks, sending plumes of water into the air. The resonating sound, akin to thunder, adds a sensory dimension to the experience.

- Timing is Everything: To experience Thunder Hole at its most dramatic, plan your visit during high tide. The best times often coincide with the two hours before high tide, creating optimal conditions for waves to surge into the cavern and produce booming sounds.
- Photography: Capture the dynamic beauty of Thunder Hole with your camera. The juxtaposition of crashing waves, sea spray, and the surrounding cliffs offers a photographic canvas that encapsulates the raw energy of the Atlantic Ocean.

Sand Beach

Nestled between the rugged cliffs of the surrounding coastline, Sand Beach stands as a pristine haven—a crescent of golden sands gently caressed by the cool waters of the Atlantic. This coastal oasis invites visitors to unwind, explore, and appreciate the harmonious union of sea and shore.

Location

Situated on the eastern shore of Mount Desert Island, Sand Beach is easily accessible via the Park Loop Road, making it a convenient stop for those exploring Acadia National Park.

How to Get There

Follow the Park Loop Road to reach Sand Beach, where ample parking is available. A short stroll from the parking area leads you to the beach, unveiling a breathtaking panorama of the Atlantic coastline.

What to Expect

As you approach Sand Beach, the juxtaposition of the vibrant blue ocean against the golden sands is a visual delight. Bordered by rocky outcrops and framed by dramatic cliffs, the beach offers a serene escape and a stark contrast to the rugged landscapes that define much of Acadia.

Things to Do

- Relax and Unwind: Spread a blanket, bask in the sun, and let the rhythmic sounds of the ocean provide a soothing soundtrack. Sand Beach is an ideal spot for relaxation, allowing visitors to unwind and appreciate the coastal beauty.
- Swimming: While the waters of the Atlantic can be brisk, especially early in the season, Sand Beach provides a refreshing opportunity for a swim. The beach's gentle slope into the ocean creates a gradual entry, suitable for both seasoned swimmers and those seeking a refreshing dip.
- Scenic Stroll: Explore the shoreline by taking a stroll along the water's edge. The juxtaposition of the smooth sands and the craggy cliffs creates a picturesque seascape that beckons exploration.
- Picnicking: Pack a picnic and enjoy a meal against the backdrop of the Atlantic. Picnic tables are available, providing a perfect spot to savor local delights while immersed in the coastal ambiance.

Otter Cliff

In the grand tapestry of Acadia's coastal wonders, Otter Cliff stands as a testament to nature's artistry—a rugged promontory that pierces the Atlantic with majestic cliffs and awe-inspiring seascapes. Perched on the eastern edge of Mount Desert Island, this iconic landmark beckons adventurers and admirers alike to behold its breathtaking vistas.

Location

Otter Cliff graces the southeastern coastline of Mount Desert Island within Acadia National Park. Accessible via Park Loop Road, it offers a commanding presence with its granite cliffs plunging dramatically into the Atlantic Ocean.

How to Get There

Follow the scenic Park Loop Road to reach the designated overlook area for Otter Cliff. Ample parking is available, allowing visitors to embark on a short walk to the cliff's edge, where panoramic views await.

What to Expect

As you approach Otter Cliff, prepare to be captivated by the sheer grandeur of its rugged cliffs. Rising approximately 110 feet above the ocean, the granite formations create a dramatic backdrop against the endless expanse of the Atlantic. The crashing waves below add a dynamic element to the scenery, creating a symphony of sights and sounds.

Things to Do

- Scenic Overlook: The designated overlook area provides an ideal vantage point to absorb the breathtaking panoramas of Otter Cliff and the surrounding coastline. Take your time to savor the beauty and contemplate the forces that shaped this coastal masterpiece.
- Photography: Otter Cliff is a photographer's paradise. Capture the changing colors of the ocean, the textured cliffs, and the interplay of light and shadow. Whether you're an amateur or seasoned photographer, the scenic vistas offer endless opportunities for captivating shots.
- Rock Climbing: For adventurous souls, Otter Cliff presents rock climbing opportunities. Experienced climbers can navigate the granite face, enjoying a unique perspective of Acadia's coastal landscapes.

Precipice Trail

For those seeking an adrenaline-pumping adventure amid Acadia's rugged terrain, the Precipice Trail stands as a thrilling ascent to panoramic heights. Carved into the granite cliffs of Champlain Mountain, this iconic trail challenges hikers with its steep pitches, iron rungs, and breathtaking views, delivering an exhilarating experience for those with a taste for adventure.

Location

The Precipice Trail is located on the eastern side of Champlain Mountain in Acadia National Park. Its trailhead is accessible from the Precipice Parking Area along the Park Loop Road.

How to Get There

Reach the Precipice Parking Area via the Park Loop Road. Due to its popularity and limited parking, arriving early is advisable. From the parking area, follow signs to the trailhead, where the adventure begins.

What to Expect

As you ascend, expect a challenging journey that rewards you with unparalleled views of Frenchman Bay, the Porcupine Islands, and the Atlantic Ocean. The trail weaves through granite cliffs, utilizing iron rungs and ladders for steep sections, creating a unique and exhilarating hiking experience.

Things to Do

- Adventurous Hiking: Embark on the Precipice Trail for an adrenaline-filled adventure. Ascend steep cliffs using iron rungs and navigate challenging sections that demand both physical prowess and mental fortitude.

- Panoramic Views: The summit of Champlain Mountain, reached through the Precipice Trail, unveils panoramic vistas that make the challenging ascent worthwhile. Take in the sweeping views of the coastline and surrounding landscapes.
- Wildlife Observation: Keep an eye out for the diverse wildlife that inhabits the area. Peregrine falcons, known for nesting on the cliffs, are a common sight. Exercise caution to avoid disturbing these magnificent birds.
- Seasonal Considerations: The Precipice Trail is typically open from mid-May to late August to protect nesting falcons. Be mindful of the seasonal closures and plan your visit accordingly to ensure both your safety and the protection of the park's wildlife.

Jordan Pond Path

In the heart of Acadia National Park, the Jordan Pond Path unfolds as a serene promenade that meanders along the shores of the pristine glacial pond. This leisurely trail encapsulates the park's natural beauty, inviting visitors to a peaceful sojourn through lush landscapes and captivating vistas.

Location

The Jordan Pond Path encircles Jordan Pond, a picturesque glacial pond situated in the central part of Mount Desert Island within Acadia National Park.

How to Get There

Access the trailhead near the Jordan Pond House, where ample parking is available. The trail forms a gentle loop around the pond, providing an accessible and scenic route for visitors of all ages.

What to Expect

Embarking on the Jordan Pond Path immerses you in the tranquility of Acadia's landscapes. The crystal-clear waters of the pond reflect the surrounding mountains, creating a mesmerizing scene. The trail itself is well-maintained, offering a comfortable stroll through diverse environments, from meadows to wooded areas.

Things to Do

- Scenic Stroll: Enjoy a stroll along the well-marked path, taking in the changing scenery. The trail is relatively flat, making it accessible for all skill levels, and offers multiple vantage points for admiring the pond and the surrounding peaks.
- Tea and Popovers at Jordan Pond House: Midway through your walk, consider a delightful break at the historic Jordan Pond House. Indulge in the tradition of afternoon tea, accompanied by the house's famous popovers, while overlooking the pond and the Bubbles mountains.
- Wildlife Observation: Jordan Pond is a haven for wildlife, and the path provides opportunities for birdwatching and observing other creatures that call the area home. Keep an eye out for waterfowl, dragonflies, and the occasional turtle basking in the sun.

Bar Harbor

Nestled on the doorstep of Acadia National Park, Bar Harbor stands as a captivating gateway to coastal charm and nautical delights. This quaint and vibrant town invites visitors to explore its historic streets, savor culinary delights, and embark on maritime adventures, creating a perfect complement to the natural wonders of Acadia.

Location

Bar Harbor is located on Mount Desert Island, just outside the eastern boundaries of Acadia National Park. It serves as a vibrant hub for visitors exploring the park and the surrounding coastal areas.

How to Get There

Accessible by car, Bar Harbor is a short drive from various entry points of Acadia National Park. The town is also a popular stop for cruise ship passengers, offering a seamless blend of coastal allure and town charm.

What to Expect

Bar Harbor exudes a captivating blend of maritime history and contemporary flair. Historic architecture lines the streets and the harbor bustles with activity. The town offers an array of shops, restaurants, and cultural attractions, creating a lively atmosphere that complements the serene landscapes of Acadia.

Things to Do

- Explore the Waterfront: Stroll along the waterfront and harbor area, where you'll encounter a mix of fishing boats, sailboats, and the iconic Bar Harbor Inn. Enjoy the maritime ambiance, and consider taking a scenic boat tour to explore the coastal beauty from a different perspective.
- Shop and Dine on Main Street: Bar Harbor's Main Street is a charming blend of boutiques, galleries, and eateries. Explore the unique shops for local crafts and souvenirs, and indulge in the diverse culinary scene, ranging from lobster shacks to fine dining establishments.
- Visit Bar Island: During low tide, venture across the sandbar to Bar Island, accessible from Bridge Street. This natural

phenomenon allows for a unique exploration of the island's trails and vistas. Be mindful of the tide schedule to ensure a safe return.

- Acadia National Park Visitor Center: Discover more about Acadia National Park at the Hulls Cove Visitor Center, located just outside Bar Harbor. Explore informative exhibits, gather trail maps, and engage with park rangers to enhance your understanding of the park's natural and cultural history.

Bass Harbor Head Lighthouse

Perched on the rugged cliffs of Mount Desert Island, the Bass Harbor Head Lighthouse stands as a stoic sentinel, guiding mariners through the swirling waters of the Atlantic. This iconic beacon, with its picturesque setting and maritime allure, is a must-visit destination within Acadia National Park.

Location

Bass Harbor Head Lighthouse is located on the southwestern tip of Mount Desert Island, overlooking the entrance to Bass Harbor. The lighthouse is situated within Acadia National Park, offering both historical charm and scenic vistas.

How to Get There

Accessing Bass Harbor Head Lighthouse is straightforward. Follow Route 102A to reach the lighthouse parking area. From there, a short and scenic trail leads to the cliffside vantage point, providing spectacular views of the lighthouse and the surrounding coastal landscapes.

What to Expect

The Bass Harbor Head Lighthouse is a quintessential New England landmark, with its white tower and red roof perched atop rugged cliffs. The setting offers a dramatic juxtaposition of the man-made structure against the natural beauty of the rocky coastline and the expansive Atlantic Ocean.

Things to Do

- Scenic Viewing: The vantage point near the lighthouse provides stunning panoramic views of the rugged coastline and the open sea. Capture the beauty of the lighthouse against the backdrop of the Atlantic, and savor the serenity of the surrounding landscapes.
- Sunset Photography: The lighthouse is particularly enchanting during sunset. Plan your visit in the evening to witness the warm hues of the setting sun casting a golden glow on the lighthouse and the coastal cliffs. It's a prime opportunity for memorable photography.
- Hiking Trails: While at the lighthouse, consider exploring nearby hiking trails, such as the Ship Harbor Trail, which winds through picturesque landscapes along the shoreline. These trails offer a closer connection to Acadia's natural wonders.

Schoodic Peninsula

While Acadia National Park's main attractions are concentrated on Mount Desert Island, the Schoodic Peninsula offers a quieter and equally captivating coastal experience. Embraced by the Atlantic, this secluded enclave boasts rocky shorelines, diverse ecosystems, and unparalleled vistas.

Location

The Schoodic Peninsula is located east of Mount Desert Island, across Frenchman Bay. Accessible by car, it provides an extension of Acadia National Park's coastal wonders.

How to Get There

Reach the Schoodic Peninsula by taking the Schoodic Loop Road, which is connected to the mainland. The approximately 8-mile scenic drive offers access to various points of interest, including stunning overlooks and hiking trails.

What to Expect

Schoodic Peninsula presents a rugged coastal landscape characterized by rocky shores, dramatic cliffs, and expansive ocean views. This less-visited part of Acadia National Park provides a serene escape, allowing visitors to connect with nature away from the crowds.

Things to Do

- Schoodic Point: At Schoodic Point, the crashing waves of the Atlantic meet the rugged cliffs, creating a dynamic seascape. The Schoodic Point Loop Trail offers a stroll along the shoreline, allowing you to immerse yourself in the coastal grandeur.
- Hiking and Biking Trails: Explore the network of hiking and biking trails that wind through the peninsula. The Anvil Trail and the Alder Trail are popular choices, offering diverse ecosystems and opportunities for birdwatching.
- Picnicking: Schoodic Peninsula provides several scenic picnic areas where you can savor a meal against the backdrop of the Atlantic. Take a moment to relax and appreciate the natural beauty that surrounds you.
- Ranger-Led Programs: Check the park schedule for ranger-led programs and activities on the Schoodic Peninsula. These programs offer educational insights into the area's natural history, wildlife, and conservation efforts.

Echo Lake

Nestled within the heart of Mount Desert Island, Echo Lake stands as a serene oasis, cradled by the surrounding hills and reflecting the tranquility of Acadia National Park. This freshwater gem invites visitors to bask in its beauty, offering opportunities for recreation and contemplation.

Location

Echo Lake is centrally located on Mount Desert Island, within Acadia National Park. Accessible by car, it provides a peaceful retreat surrounded by the park's diverse landscapes.

How to Get There

Follow signs and access the Echo Lake Beach area from Route 102. Ample parking is available, allowing easy access to the lake's shoreline and recreational facilities.

What to Expect

Echo Lake exudes a calm and inviting ambiance. The freshwater lake is surrounded by lush greenery and hills, creating a picturesque setting that invites visitors to unwind. The clear waters of the lake provide an opportunity for various recreational activities and a refreshing escape from the coastal landscapes.

Things to Do

- Swimming: Echo Lake's sandy beach is an ideal spot for a refreshing swim. The clear and cool waters of the lake beckon visitors to enjoy a leisurely dip, making it a popular destination during warmer months.
- Picnicking: Take advantage of the designated picnic areas and enjoy a meal surrounded by the natural beauty of Echo Lake. Pack

a picnic and savor the tranquility while appreciating the views of the lake and surrounding hills.

- Canoeing and Kayaking: Explore the lake from a different perspective by canoeing or kayaking on its calm waters. Bring your watercraft or rent one locally to embark on a peaceful journey surrounded by nature.
- Hiking Trails: Echo Lake provides access to nearby hiking trails, including the Beech Mountain Trail. Embark on a hike to gain elevated views of the lake and the surrounding landscapes, adding an extra layer of exploration to your visit.

Bubble Rock

Perched precariously on the edge of South Bubble Mountain, Bubble Rock is a geological curiosity that defies gravity. This iconic glacial erratic, seemingly teetering on the brink, offers a unique blend of natural wonder and panoramic views, making it a must-see attraction in Acadia National Park.

Location

Bubble Rock is situated on South Bubble Mountain, one of the peaks in the central part of Mount Desert Island within Acadia National Park. Accessible by hiking trails, it provides a rewarding destination for those seeking both natural wonders and scenic vistas.

How to Get There

Reach Bubble Rock by hiking the South Bubble Trail. The trailhead is located near Jordan Pond House, and the relatively short hike offers a moderate challenge with a rewarding payoff at the summit.

What to Expect

Bubble Rock commands attention with its striking appearance—a massive glacial erratic balanced precariously on the exposed ledge of

South Bubble Mountain. The surrounding landscape offers breathtaking views of Jordan Pond and the distant mountains, adding to the allure of this geological marvel.

Things to Do

- Hiking to Bubble Rock: Embark on the South Bubble Trail to reach the summit and encounter Bubble Rock up close. The trail winds through wooded areas and unveils expansive views as you approach the unique geological formation.
- Photography: Capture the surreal sight of Bubble Rock against the backdrop of Acadia's landscapes. The panoramic views from the summit provide a stunning setting for photography, especially during sunrise or sunset.
- Enjoying Scenic Vistas: While Bubble Rock is the main attraction, the summit of South Bubble Mountain offers panoramic vistas of Jordan Pond, the Bubbles, and the surrounding peaks. Take time to savor the views and appreciate the diverse landscapes that define Acadia National Park.
- Connecting Trails: Extend your hiking adventure by exploring nearby trails, such as the Jordan Pond Path or the North Bubble Trail. Each trail offers unique perspectives and opportunities to delve deeper into the natural beauty of the area.

Isle au Haut

For those seeking a more secluded and immersive experience within Acadia National Park, Isle au Haut beckons as a wilderness retreat beyond the mainland. This remote island, accessible by ferry, offers pristine landscapes, hiking trails, and a chance to reconnect with nature in its purest form.

Location

Isle au Haut is an island located off the coast of Stonington, Maine, accessible by ferry from Stonington or seasonal ferry service from Acadia National Park's main visitor centers.

How to Get There

Take a ferry from Stonington to Isle au Haut, where you can explore the island's natural beauty and hiking trails. Ferry services operate seasonally, and it's advisable to check schedules and availability in advance.

What to Expect

Isle au Haut stands as a haven for wilderness enthusiasts. The island is characterized by rugged shorelines, dense forests, and a network of hiking trails that lead to secluded coves and panoramic viewpoints. With limited services, Isle au Haut offers a pristine and unspoiled escape.

Things to Do

- Hiking Trails: Explore the island's hiking trails, such as the Cliff Trail or the Duck Harbor Mountain Trail. These trails lead to elevated viewpoints, providing sweeping vistas of the Atlantic, neighboring islands, and the rugged coastline.
- Biking and Kayaking: Rent a bike or kayak to explore the island's scenic beauty from a different perspective. The quiet roads and sheltered coves make Isle au Haut an ideal destination for outdoor activities.
- Wildlife Observation: The island is home to diverse wildlife, including seabirds, deer, and seals. Birdwatchers will appreciate the opportunity to observe migratory and resident species in this natural habitat.

- Primitive Camping: For those seeking a more immersive experience, Isle au Haut offers primitive camping opportunities. Permits are required, and camping is limited to designated areas, ensuring minimal impact on the island's ecosystems.

Wonderland Trail

In the southwestern part of Mount Desert Island, Wonderland Trail unfolds as a coastal marvel, inviting visitors to wander through diverse ecosystems and witness the dynamic interplay of land and sea. This leisurely trail provides an accessible exploration of Acadia's coastal treasures.

Location

Wonderland Trail is located near the southern tip of Mount Desert Island, within Acadia National Park. Accessible by car, it offers a relatively easy and scenic hike for visitors of all ages.

How to Get There

Access Wonderland Trail by following Route 102A to reach the parking area. From there, a well-marked trail leads through lush woodlands and unveils the wonders of the coastal environment.

What to Expect

Wonderland Trail lives up to its name, offering a magical journey through coastal landscapes. The trail winds through mossy forests, tidal flats, and rugged shores, providing glimpses of tidal pools and panoramic views of the ocean.

Things to Do

- Coastal Exploration: The trail takes you through diverse coastal environments, allowing you to explore tidal flats, rocky shores, and picturesque coves. Take your time to investigate tidal pools and observe the marine life that thrives in this unique ecosystem.

- Birdwatching: Wonderland Trail is a haven for birdwatchers. The coastal habitats attract a variety of seabirds, shorebirds, and songbirds. Bring binoculars to enhance your birdwatching experience and appreciate the avian diversity.
- Photography: Capture the natural beauty of Acadia's coastline with your camera. The trail offers numerous scenic spots, from rocky outcrops overlooking the ocean to the intricate details of tidal pool life.

Park Loop Road

Park Loop Road serves as the scenic artery that winds through the heart of Acadia National Park, connecting visitors to a myriad of breathtaking landscapes, iconic landmarks, and opportunities for exploration. This renowned road offers a panoramic odyssey, revealing the diverse beauty that defines Acadia.

Location

Park Loop Road traverses the central and coastal regions of Mount Desert Island within Acadia National Park. The road provides access to various trailheads, viewpoints, and attractions.

How to Get There

Access Park Loop Road from the Hulls Cove Visitor Center or the Bar Harbor entrance. The road is well-marked, and a park pass is required for entry. During the peak season, a portion of the road is one-way, providing a seamless flow of traffic.

What to Expect

Park Loop Road unfolds as a visual tapestry, showcasing Acadia's rich diversity. From wooded landscapes and rocky shores to elevated vistas, the road encapsulates the essence of the park's natural and cultural heritage.

Things to Do

- Scenic Overlooks: Park Loop Road features numerous scenic overlooks that provide breathtaking views of the Atlantic Ocean, Frenchman Bay, and the surrounding mountains. Take advantage of these viewpoints to capture the beauty of Acadia through your lens.
- Jordan Pond House: The road passes near the historic Jordan Pond House, offering a delightful spot for afternoon tea and popovers. Take a break, enjoy the culinary delights, and appreciate the views of Jordan Pond.
- Thunder Hole and Sand Beach: Park Loop Road provides access to popular attractions like Thunder Hole and Sand Beach. These natural wonders showcase the power of the ocean and the pristine beauty of Acadia's coastline.
- Carriage Roads and Trailheads: Numerous trailheads and entrances to the carriage road system are accessible from Park Loop Road. Explore the diverse hiking and biking opportunities that radiate from the road, allowing you to delve deeper into Acadia's landscapes.

Chapter 4

Must-Do Activities

Hiking Trails

Acadia National Park is a hiker's paradise, boasting a diverse network of trails that traverse mountains, meander along rocky shores, and lead to breathtaking vistas. Whether you're an experienced trekker seeking a challenging ascent or a casual stroller in search of scenic beauty, Acadia's hiking trails offer an array of options for all skill levels.

Cadillac Mountain South Ridge Trail

Embark on the iconic South Ridge Trail to ascend the tallest peak on the East Coast, Cadillac Mountain. This moderate to strenuous trail winds through forested terrain, revealing glimpses of panoramic views before reaching the summit. As you ascend, the landscape transforms from wooded slopes to exposed granite, culminating in an expansive vista atop Cadillac's peak. Sunrise hikes are particularly enchanting, offering a front-row seat to the first rays of light gracing the United States each morning.

Precipice Trail

For those seeking an adrenaline-pumping adventure, the Precipice Trail beckons with its challenging ascent up the granite cliffs of Champlain Mountain. Fitted with iron rungs and ladders, this trail is not for the faint of heart. The reward? Sweeping views of Frenchman Bay and the Atlantic Ocean. Open from mid-May to late August to protect nesting falcons, the Precipice Trail combines the thrill of rock climbing with the beauty of Acadia's coastal landscapes.

Jordan Pond Path

Offering a more serene hiking experience, the Jordan Pond Path invites visitors to circumnavigate the pristine glacial pond. This easy trail boasts a well-maintained path, making it accessible to hikers of all ages. As you walk, the crystal-clear waters of Jordan Pond reflect the surrounding mountains, creating a picturesque setting. The trail also passes the historic Jordan Pond House, where you can indulge in afternoon tea and popovers, adding a culinary delight to your hiking excursion.

Wonderland Trail

For coastal exploration on foot, the Wonderland Trail unfolds as a leisurely pathway through diverse ecosystems. Meandering through tidal flats, mossy forests, and rocky shores, this trail showcases the dynamic interplay of land and sea. Coastal wonders such as tidal pools and seabird habitats dot the landscape, creating a captivating journey that immerses hikers in Acadia's coastal marvels.

Biking Adventures

Biking enthusiasts will find Acadia National Park to be a haven of scenic routes, carriage roads, and challenging trails. Whether you prefer a leisurely ride along the coastline or a more adrenaline-fueled mountain biking experience, Acadia's biking adventures cater to riders of various skill levels.

Carriage Roads

Designed by John D. Rockefeller Jr., Acadia's carriage roads offer a network of well-maintained trails ideal for biking. These gravel paths wind through picturesque landscapes, passing stone bridges, meandering streams, and dense forests. With approximately 45 miles of carriage roads to explore, bikers can tailor their journey to match their desired level of difficulty and scenery.

Park Loop Road

For those who prefer cycling on paved roads with stunning vistas, Park Loop Road provides a scenic cycling odyssey through the heart of Acadia. Bikers can enjoy breathtaking views of the Atlantic Ocean, Frenchman Bay, and iconic landmarks like Thunder Hole and Sand Beach. With multiple overlooks and points of interest along the way, cyclists can immerse themselves in the diverse beauty that defines Acadia National Park.

Mountain Biking on Carriage Roads

Thrill-seekers can venture onto selected carriage roads that allow mountain biking. While not all carriage roads permit biking, those that do offer an adrenaline-fueled experience amid nature's splendor. Tackling the undulating terrain and navigating the twists and turns of these designated paths provides a unique perspective of Acadia's landscapes for avid mountain bikers.

Schoodic Peninsula

Extend your biking adventures beyond Mount Desert Island to the Schoodic Peninsula. The approximately 8-mile Schoodic Loop Road provides a tranquil and scenic route for cyclists. This less-visited enclave of Acadia National Park offers a different coastal experience, allowing bikers to explore rocky shorelines, enjoy panoramic views, and savor the serenity of this secluded peninsula.

Bird Watching

Acadia National Park's diverse ecosystems provide a haven for birdwatchers, offering a rich tapestry of avian life against the backdrop of coastal landscapes and wooded expanses. From soaring raptors to delicate songbirds, Acadia's birdwatching opportunities invite enthusiasts of all levels to witness the intricate dance of wings and melodies in the heart of nature.

Sieur de Monts Spring

Begin your birdwatching adventure at Sieur de Monts Spring, where the mellifluous tunes of songbirds fill the air. This tranquil area, located near the park's visitor center, is a prime location for observing warblers, thrushes, and other migratory birds. Bring your binoculars and listen to the symphony of nature as you explore the wooded trails surrounding the spring.

Wonderland Trail

The Wonderland Trail, known for its coastal marvels, also offers a unique birdwatching experience. Coastal habitats attract a variety of seabirds, shorebirds, and migratory species. Scan the rocky shores and tidal flats for opportunities to spot cormorants, gulls, and the occasional bald eagle. The rhythmic sounds of the waves provide a soothing backdrop to your birdwatching excursion.

Jordan Pond

For waterfowl enthusiasts, Jordan Pond provides an idyllic setting for birdwatching. The pristine waters reflect the nearby mountains, establishing a tranquil atmosphere. Keep an eye out for common loons, mergansers, and other water-loving birds. The combination of mountain scenery and waterfowl activity makes Jordan Pond a picturesque location for observing avian life.

Cadillac Mountain

Elevate your birdwatching experience by heading to the summit of Cadillac Mountain. As the tallest peak on the East Coast, Cadillac offers a vantage point for observing raptors in flight. During migration seasons, you may witness the impressive spectacle of hawks, eagles, and falcons soaring above, riding the thermals as they navigate the skies. Bring a spotting scope to enhance your view of these majestic birds.

Whale Watching Tours

Embark on a maritime adventure off the coast of Acadia National Park with whale-watching tours that promise encounters with some of the ocean's most majestic inhabitants. From the comfort of a boat, visitors can witness the awe-inspiring displays of whales breaching, dolphins playing, and other marine life thriving in the nutrient-rich waters of the Gulf of Maine.

Bar Harbor Whale Watch Co

Join a whale watching tour with Bar Harbor Whale Watch Co. for an unforgettable journey into the realm of marine giants. Knowledgeable naturalists guide passengers through the Gulf of Maine, providing insights into the behaviors and biology of whales. Keep a lookout for humpback whales, minke whales, and the iconic fin whales, which frequent these waters. The tours also offer opportunities to spot porpoises, seals, and a variety of seabirds.

Diver Ed's Dive-In Theater

For a unique and educational whale-watching experience, consider Diver Ed's Dive-In Theater. Led by marine biologist Ed Monat, these tours blend entertainment with scientific insights. Dive-In Theater's underwater video feeds and live commentary enhance the understanding of marine life, making it an engaging experience for all ages. From the comfort of the boat, passengers can marvel at the grace and power of whales in their natural habitat.

Lulu Lobster Boat Ride

Combine the thrill of whale watching with the charm of a lobster boat excursion aboard the Lulu Lobster Boat Ride. As you cruise through Frenchman Bay, knowledgeable guides share information about local marine life, including whales and seals. The tour also includes a demonstration of lobster fishing techniques, providing a well-rounded maritime experience. Witnessing whales against the backdrop of Acadia's coastal beauty adds an extra layer of excitement to this nautical adventure.

Acadia Puffin Cruise

Explore the waters around Acadia National Park with an Acadia Puffin Cruise, offering the chance to encounter not only whales but also seabirds, seals, and other marine creatures. Naturalists on board provide insights into the region's ecology and marine conservation efforts. The cruise may bring you face-to-face with playful dolphins or the majestic sight of a whale's tail breaking the surface. Seize the opportunity to capture these moments with your camera for lasting memories.

Stargazing Events

As the sun sets over Acadia National Park, a celestial spectacle unfolds in the night sky. Away from city lights, Acadia offers stargazers a front-row seat to the wonders of the cosmos. Joining stargazing events within the park enhances the experience, providing insights from astronomers and an opportunity to marvel at the vastness of the universe.

Star Parties with Acadia Night Sky Festival

The Acadia Night Sky Festival hosts annual star parties, inviting visitors to gather in designated areas for an enchanting evening under the stars. Expert astronomers guide participants through the constellations, planets, and other celestial wonders visible in Acadia's pristine night sky. Bring a telescope or simply lay out a blanket and revel in the beauty of a natural planetarium.

Jordan Pond Evenings

Experience the magic of stargazing at Jordan Pond. On clear nights, the tranquil waters reflect the brilliance of the night sky, creating a captivating scene. Join organized events or venture to the shores with your telescope to observe constellations, planets, and, if the timing is right, meteor showers. The juxtaposition of Acadia's landscapes and the celestial realm provides a unique and awe-inspiring experience.

Cadillac Mountain Summit

For an elevated stargazing experience, venture to the summit of Cadillac Mountain. The highest point on the East Coast offers unobstructed views of the night sky. Attend ranger-led programs or join fellow enthusiasts for organized stargazing events. With minimal light pollution, Cadillac Mountain provides an ideal vantage point for observing the moon, planets, and distant galaxies.

Tips for Stargazing in Acadia

- Dark Sky Protocol: To enhance the stargazing experience, embrace dark sky protocols. Minimize the use of artificial lights, use red filters on flashlights to preserve night vision, and choose clothing and gear with minimal reflective surfaces.
- Timing: Check the schedule for organized stargazing events during your visit. Plan your stargazing activities during new moon phases for optimal visibility of celestial objects.
- Binoculars and Telescopes: While not mandatory, bringing binoculars or a portable telescope can enhance your ability to observe details such as lunar craters, planetary features, and distant star clusters.

Water Activities

Surrounded by the Atlantic Ocean, Acadia National Park offers a myriad of water-based activities for enthusiasts seeking maritime adventures. From tranquil explorations of freshwater lakes to exhilarating encounters with the open sea, Acadia's water activities cater to a range of preferences and skill levels.

Kayaking on Jordan Pond

Embrace the serenity of Acadia's landscapes by kayaking on Jordan Pond. The clear and calm waters of the pond provide an ideal setting for a leisurely paddle. Bring your kayak or rent one locally to explore the shoreline, enjoy views of the Bubbles mountains, and experience the tranquility of this iconic freshwater destination.

Sea Kayaking Tours

For a more adventurous kayaking experience, consider joining a sea kayaking tour along Acadia's rugged coastline. Guided tours, led by experienced instructors, provide an opportunity to explore sea caves, navigate among rocky outcrops, and witness coastal wildlife. From seals sunning on rocks to seabirds soaring overhead, sea kayaking offers a unique perspective of Acadia's maritime wonders.

Sand Beach

Sand Beach, nestled between rocky headlands, offers an ideal setting for water enthusiasts seeking a coastal escape. While swimming in the chilly Atlantic waters is invigorating, Sand Beach is also a popular destination for surfing. Experienced surfers can catch the waves breaking along the shore, adding an element of exhilaration to their coastal visit.

Whale Watching and Boat Tours

Expand your maritime adventures with boat tours and whale-watching excursions. Join a boat tour to explore the coastal beauty of Acadia, from secluded coves to towering cliffs. Whale-watching tours offer the chance to witness the majestic giants of the ocean, including humpback whales, minke whales, and porpoises. The open sea becomes a theater of marine life, providing an immersive experience for participants.

Nature Photography

Acadia National Park's landscapes, from towering peaks to coastal wonders, provide a visual feast for nature photographers. Whether you're a seasoned professional or an amateur with a smartphone, Acadia's natural splendors offer endless opportunities to capture timeless moments and create lasting memories through the lens.

Sunrise at Cadillac Mountain

Begin your photographic journey by capturing the sunrise from the summit of Cadillac Mountain. As the highest point along the East Coast, Cadillac offers a panoramic view of the surrounding landscapes bathed in the warm hues of the morning sun. Plan your visit during clear mornings to witness the breathtaking transition from darkness to dawn, creating a canvas of colors that paint the mountains and ocean.

Jordan Pond Reflections

Jordan Pond, with its clear waters and iconic views of the Bubbles Mountains, provides an ideal setting for capturing reflections. Visit during calm mornings or evenings when the water mirrors the surrounding landscapes, creating compositions that showcase the harmony of mountains, trees, and sky. The juxtaposition of nature's elements makes Jordan Pond a captivating subject for photographers.

Thunder Hole Drama

For dynamic and dramatic shots, head to Thunder Hole during high tide. As waves crash against the coastal rocks, water surges into a cavern, creating a resounding boom. Capture the power and energy of the ocean against the backdrop of Acadia's rugged coastline. Timing is crucial, so check tide schedules for optimal photography conditions.

Bass Harbor Head Lighthouse

Bass Harbor Head Lighthouse, perched on the southwestern cliffs of Mount Desert Island, is an iconic subject for maritime photography. The classic white tower against the backdrop of the Atlantic Ocean and rugged shores creates a timeless and elegant scene. Plan your visit during golden hours to capture the lighthouse bathed in the soft glow of sunrise or sunset.

Ranger-Led Programs

For visitors seeking a deeper understanding of Acadia's natural and cultural heritage, ranger-led programs offer educational adventures led by knowledgeable park rangers. These programs provide insights into the park's ecology, wildlife, geology, and history, enriching your overall experience and fostering a deeper connection with Acadia.

Guided Nature Walks

Join a guided nature walk led by a park ranger to explore the diverse ecosystems of Acadia. Rangers share their expertise on local flora and fauna, providing information on plant identification, wildlife behavior, and the ecological significance of the park. Nature walks are suitable for all ages and offer a leisurely pace for observation and photography.

Evening Campfire Programs

Gather around the campfire for evening programs led by rangers, where stories of Acadia's natural wonders and cultural history come to life. Learn about the park's geology, Native American heritage, and conservation efforts. These programs often include stargazing sessions, adding an astronomical dimension to the storytelling experience.

Birdwatching Workshops

Participate in ranger-led birdwatching workshops to enhance your understanding of Acadia's avian residents. Rangers share insights into bird behavior, habitats, and the diverse species that call the park home. Whether you're a novice birdwatcher or an experienced enthusiast, these workshops offer an opportunity to hone your skills and appreciate the rich birdlife of Acadia.

History and Culture Talks

Delve into Acadia's history and cultural heritage through ranger-led talks and presentations. Learn about the park's establishment, the evolution of its landscapes, and the people who have shaped its legacy. These programs provide a holistic view of Acadia's significance, bridging the past with the present and fostering a greater appreciation for its diverse heritage.

Camping Experiences

For those seeking a more immersive and nocturnal connection with Acadia National Park, camping experiences offer the opportunity to sleep under the stars, surrounded by the park's natural beauty. From established campgrounds to more primitive backcountry sites, Acadia provides diverse options for camping enthusiasts.

Blackwoods Campground

Nestled among the pines, Blackwoods Campground offers a tranquil setting for camping amid Acadia's wilderness. With its proximity to popular trailheads, including the Cadillac South Ridge Trail, Blackwoods is an ideal base for hikers. Enjoy the serenity of nature, the rustling of leaves, and the possibility of stargazing from your campsite. Be sure to secure reservations, especially during peak seasons.

Seawall Campground

For a camping experience with a coastal touch, Seawall Campground is located near the southwestern shores of Mount Desert Island. Campsites here offer a more secluded atmosphere, surrounded by the natural sounds of the ocean. The campground's proximity to Wonderland Trail and Ship Harbor Nature Trail makes it an excellent choice for those seeking coastal exploration during the day and a peaceful night's rest.

Primitive Camping on Isle au Haut

For the adventurous spirits, consider primitive camping on Isle au Haut, Acadia's remote island. Obtain the necessary permits and take a ferry to the island for a back-to-basics camping experience. Set up camp amidst the island's pristine landscapes, surrounded by dense forests and the rhythmic sounds of the Atlantic. Primitive camping on Isle au Haut is an opportunity to disconnect and immerse yourself in the untouched beauty of Acadia.

Tips for Camping in Acadia

- Reservations: During peak seasons, it's advisable to make campground reservations in advance, especially for popular sites like Blackwoods and Seawall.

- Leave No Trace: Adhere to Leave No Trace principles to minimize your impact on the environment. Pack out all waste, respect wildlife, and follow designated trails to preserve the park's natural integrity.
- Night Sky Enjoyment: Take advantage of the dark skies in Acadia for stargazing. Bring a telescope or simply lay out under the stars for a celestial experience.

Carriage Road Explorations

John D. Rockefeller Jr.'s vision for a network of carriage roads in Acadia has created a unique opportunity for exploration by bike or foot. These gravel pathways wind through picturesque landscapes, crossing bridges and skirting ponds, providing a delightful and historic way to experience the park.

Carriage Road Biking

The carriage roads offer approximately 45 miles of biking opportunities, with routes suitable for riders of various skill levels. Traverse through wooded areas, past stone bridges, and alongside streams, enjoying the serene landscapes that unfold along the way. Carriage road biking provides a chance to appreciate the historic vision of Rockefeller while immersing yourself in Acadia's natural beauty.

Walking and Hiking on Carriage Roads

While the carriage roads are renowned for biking, they also offer tranquil pathways for walkers and hikers. Explore the network of trails that wind through woodlands and open into scenic clearings. Consider a leisurely walk around Jordan Pond on the carriage road that circles the pond, providing stunning views of the Bubbles mountains and the tranquil waters.

Carriage Road Highlights

As you explore the carriage roads, take note of the unique stone bridges that span streams and ravines. Each bridge is a testament to Rockefeller's commitment to blending human-made structures with the natural environment. Additionally, visit landmarks like the Jordan Pond Gatehouse and the Wildwood Stables to appreciate the historical significance of these structures within the park.

Ranger-Led Carriage Road Programs

Enhance your carriage road experience by participating in ranger-led programs focused on these historic pathways. Rangers provide insights into the construction, history, and natural features of the carriage roads. Joining a guided program adds depth to your exploration, offering a greater appreciation for the cultural and ecological aspects of these iconic routes.

Rock Climbing

For adrenaline-seekers and climbing enthusiasts, Acadia National Park offers a unique opportunity to explore vertical landscapes through rock climbing. With its rugged cliffs and granite formations, Acadia provides a thrilling playground for climbers of various skill levels.

Otter Cliffs

Otter Cliffs, rising dramatically from the Atlantic Ocean, is a premier destination for sea cliff climbing. The granite cliffs provide challenging routes with breathtaking views of the ocean below. Climbers can tackle routes of varying difficulty, and the sound of crashing waves adds a dynamic and immersive element to the climbing experience. Due to the tidal nature of Otter Cliffs, climbers are advised to check tide charts and plan their ascents accordingly.

Precipice Trail

For those seeking a mix of hiking and climbing, the Precipice Trail on Champlain Mountain offers a thrilling ascent with sections of iron rungs and ladders. The trail is open seasonally to protect nesting peregrine falcons, providing a unique climbing experience amid the stunning coastal landscapes of Acadia.

Jordan Cliffs

Located on the east face of Penobscot Mountain, Jordan Cliffs presents climbers with challenging granite walls and panoramic views of Jordan Pond and the surrounding landscapes. Climbing routes on Jordan Cliffs range from moderate to advanced, providing options for climbers with varying skill levels. The alpine setting adds an extra layer of beauty to this rock-climbing destination.

Climbing Safety and Guidelines

- Guided Climbing Programs: Consider joining guided climbing programs led by experienced instructors. These programs not only provide valuable instruction but also enhance safety by ensuring proper equipment use and adherence to climbing guidelines.
- Equipment Inspection: Ensure that your climbing equipment, including harnesses, helmets, and ropes, is in good condition. Regularly inspect gear for any signs of wear and tear.
- Weather Awareness: Stay informed about weather conditions, as rock climbing is weather-dependent. Sudden changes in weather can impact climbing safety, and it's crucial to prioritize your well-being.

Guided Tours

For visitors who prefer expert guidance and local insights, guided tours in Acadia National Park provide a curated and educational experience. Knowledgeable guides lead participants through the park's iconic landmarks, sharing stories of natural and cultural significance.

Acadia National Park Tours

Joining general park tours offers a comprehensive exploration of Acadia's highlights. Expert guides provide commentary on the park's geology, flora, fauna, and history. Whether you're traveling by bus, van, or on foot, these tours offer a convenient way to cover key points of interest while gaining in-depth knowledge from seasoned interpreters.

Photography Tours

Photography enthusiasts can opt for guided tours tailored to capturing the park's scenic beauty. Led by photography experts familiar with Acadia's best vantage points and lighting conditions, these tours provide tips and techniques to enhance your photographic skills. From sunrise at Cadillac Mountain to the coastal vistas of Thunder Hole, photography tours offer a creative and educational exploration of Acadia.

Birdwatching Excursions

For birdwatching enthusiasts, guided birdwatching tours led by experienced naturalists offer an opportunity to discover Acadia's diverse avian life. Learn to identify different species, understand their behaviors, and explore the park's birding hotspots. Guided birdwatching tours enhance the birdwatching experience with insights and knowledge from knowledgeable guides.

Customized Adventure Tours

Consider booking customized adventure tours that cater to specific interests and activities. Whether you're interested in hiking, kayaking, or a combination of outdoor pursuits, specialized guides can tailor an itinerary to match your preferences. These personalized tours provide a flexible and immersive way to experience Acadia National Park.

Cultural Events

Acadia National Park not only showcases natural wonders but also celebrates its rich cultural heritage through various events and programs. Immerse yourself in the cultural tapestry of the park by participating in events that highlight its history, traditions, and the communities that have shaped its legacy.

Acadia Night Sky Festival

Join the annual Acadia Night Sky Festival, a cultural event that blends science, art, and community celebration. This multi-day festival features stargazing events, night sky photography workshops, and presentations by astronomers. Engage with experts, witness the magic of the night sky, and participate in the festivities that celebrate Acadia's designation as a Dark Sky Park.

Native American Heritage Celebration

Discover the Native American heritage of the region by participating in events that showcase indigenous traditions, crafts, and storytelling. Learn about the Wabanaki peoples' deep connection to the land and the significance of Acadia in their cultural narratives. Native American heritage celebrations provide an opportunity to gain insights into the cultural diversity that enriches Acadia's history.

Historical Talks and Tours

Attend historical talks and guided tours led by interpreters and historians to delve into Acadia's past. Explore the park's role in conservation, the construction of carriage roads by John D. Rockefeller Jr., and the evolution of Acadia's landscapes. Cultural events that focus on history provide a deeper understanding of the human impact on the park and the efforts to preserve its natural beauty.

Art Exhibitions and Workshops

Engage with the artistic side of Acadia by attending art exhibitions and workshops inspired by the park's landscapes. Local artists often draw inspiration from Acadia's beauty, and cultural events centered around art provide an opportunity to appreciate creative expressions that capture the essence of the park.

Shopping in Bar Harbor

While Acadia National Park offers pristine natural landscapes, the nearby town of Bar Harbor provides a charming backdrop for shopping excursions. Explore the streets lined with unique boutiques, galleries, and artisan shops, offering a diverse array of items that reflect the coastal charm of this quintessential New England town.

Bar Harbor Shops

Discover locally crafted treasures, including handmade jewelry, artwork, and souvenirs, in the shops scattered throughout Bar Harbor. Many artisans draw inspiration from Acadia's landscapes, creating pieces that serve as meaningful mementos of your visit. Explore Main Street and Cottage Street for a delightful shopping experience.

Coastal Cuisine Markets

Indulge in the culinary offerings of Bar Harbor by exploring coastal cuisine markets. Sample locally sourced products, including fresh seafood, artisanal cheeses, and gourmet treats. These markets not only provide an opportunity to taste the flavors of the region but also offer unique items that make for delightful souvenirs or gifts.

Outdoor Gear Outfitters

For those seeking outdoor gear or Acadia-themed apparel, Bar Harbor is home to outdoor outfitters that cater to adventurers. Find quality gear, comfortable clothing, and accessories designed for exploration in Acadia National Park. Whether you're gearing up for a hike or simply want a stylish reminder of your outdoor experiences, these outfitters have you covered.

Bar Harbor Village Green

Visit the Bar Harbor Village Green, a central gathering place that hosts seasonal markets and festivals. These events showcase local artisans, farmers, and craftsmen, offering an immersive shopping experience in the heart of Bar Harbor. Explore the vibrant atmosphere, discover unique products, and engage with the community during these festive occasions.

Wildlife Safaris

Embark on wildlife safaris to explore the diverse fauna that calls Acadia National Park home. From coastal birds to elusive mammals, these guided excursions provide an opportunity to observe and learn about the park's rich biodiversity.

Birding Safaris

Join birding safaris led by experienced naturalists to discover the wealth of birdlife within Acadia. From migratory songbirds to coastal raptors, these safaris offer a chance to observe birds in their natural habitats. Learn about bird behavior, migration patterns, and the importance of Acadia as a haven for avian species.

Seal Watching Tours

Embark on seal-watching tours to witness the playful antics of harbor seals and gray seals along Acadia's shores. Knowledgeable guides provide insights into the behavior and ecology of these marine mammals. The tours often explore coastal areas where seals haul out, providing a unique opportunity to observe them in their natural environment.

Wildlife Photography Safaris

For photography enthusiasts, wildlife photography safaris offer a chance to capture stunning images of Acadia's fauna. Guides with knowledge of the park's hotspots for wildlife sightings lead participants to areas frequented by deer, foxes, and other mammals. Bring your camera and lenses for an immersive wildlife photography experience.

Night Sky Safaris

Explore the nocturnal wonders of Acadia with night sky safaris that focus on celestial events and astronomy. Led by astronomers or naturalists, these safaris provide an opportunity to stargaze and witness phenomena such as meteor showers, celestial alignments, and the brilliance of the Milky Way. Discover the park's dark sky beauty and the celestial tapestry above.

Chapter 5

Dining in Acadia

Acadia National Park not only captivates with its natural beauty but also offers a delightful culinary experience that complements the coastal charm of the region. As you explore the park's wonders, embark on a culinary journey that showcases the best of local flavors, with a particular focus on seafood delights and the richness of the area's local cuisine.

Seafood Delights

Jordan Pond House

Nestled beside the serene waters of Jordan Pond, the historic Jordan Pond House stands as an iconic dining destination within Acadia National Park. Indulge in the richness of Maine's lobster culture with their signature Lobster Stew. Served with a side of popovers, this elegant dish features succulent lobster meat in a creamy broth, creating a harmonious blend of flavors. The picturesque views of the pond add to the enchantment, making it a must-visit for seafood enthusiasts. Expect to spend around $28 for this delectable experience.

Thurston's Lobster Pound

For a more laid-back, quintessentially Maine experience, head to Thurston's Lobster Pound in Bernard. This seafood haven offers the classic Lobster Roll, a generous portion of freshly picked lobster meat, lightly seasoned, and nestled in a buttered and toasted roll. The straightforward preparation allows the sweet and tender flavor of the lobster to shine. With picnic tables overlooking the harbor, Thurston's provides an authentic lobster shack experience. The Lobster Roll is priced at approximately $22, making it an affordable and delicious treat.

Beal's Lobster Pier

Located on Mount Desert Island, Beal's Lobster Pier is celebrated for its seafood variety and stunning waterfront views. Dive into their Crab-Stuffed Haddock, a dish that showcases the marriage of local crabmeat and fresh haddock. Baked to perfection and drizzled with a lemon-butter sauce, this seafood creation exemplifies the culinary craftsmanship of the region. The Crab-Stuffed Haddock is priced around $28, offering a delectable taste of the ocean's bounty.

Abel's Lobster Pound

Situated in picturesque Somes Sound, Abel's Lobster Pound provides not only panoramic views but also an unforgettable dining experience. Opt for their Lobster Dinner, featuring a whole Maine lobster served with sides like corn on the cob and coleslaw. Abel's commitment to freshness ensures a sumptuous and authentic taste of Maine's signature crustacean. The Lobster Dinner at Abel's is priced at approximately $38, providing a memorable feast against the backdrop of scenic coastal beauty.

Local Cuisine

The Burning Tree

For a taste of local cuisine that goes beyond seafood, The Burning Tree in Otter Creek offers homestyle Maine comfort food. Try their Blueberry Pancakes, a breakfast delight made with fresh Maine blueberries. The fluffy pancakes, drizzled with Maine maple syrup, provide a sweet and savory start to the day. The Blueberry Pancakes at The Burning Tree are priced at around $12, delivering a delicious embrace of Maine's agricultural bounty.

Side Street Café

Located in Bar Harbor, the Side Street Café is celebrated for its casual atmosphere and commitment to using locally sourced ingredients. Dive into the essence of Maine with their Wild Blueberry Muffins. Bursting with the intense flavor of wild blueberries, these muffins showcase the region's agricultural abundance. Paired with a cup of locally roasted coffee, this delightful treat is priced at around $3, making it a perfect snack or breakfast option for those exploring Bar Harbor's streets.

Trenton Bridge Lobster Pound

For a unique twist on local cuisine, visit Trenton Bridge Lobster Pound. While renowned for its lobster offerings, the lobster pound also features Maine Potato Skins as a flavorful side. Savor the taste of Maine-grown potatoes, loaded with cheese, bacon, and sour cream. This dish provides a delightful blend of comfort and local authenticity. The Maine Potato Skins are priced at approximately $8, offering a savory complement to your seafood indulgences.

2 Cats Restaurant

Situated in Bar Harbor, 2 Cats Restaurant adds a touch of innovation to classic Maine breakfast fare. Try their Cranberry Walnut French Toast, a decadent creation featuring thick slices of French toast adorned with cranberries and walnuts. Drizzled with Maine maple syrup, this dish combines sweet, savory, and nutty flavors for a delightful breakfast experience. The Cranberry Walnut French Toast is priced at around $14, providing a unique and satisfying start to your day.

Fine Dining

The Terrace Grille

Perched on the cliffs of Mount Desert Island, The Terrace Grille at the Bar Harbor Inn offers an exquisite fine dining experience. Revel in the ambiance of Victorian elegance while savoring dishes crafted with precision and creativity. Signature offerings include the Pan-Seared Scallops with Lemon Beurre Blanc and the Herb-Crusted Rack of Lamb. With an extensive wine list to complement your meal, The Terrace Grille provides a refined culinary escapade. Prices for fine dining dishes at The Terrace Grille range from $30 to $60, offering an indulgent experience for discerning palates.

Mache Bistro

In the heart of Bar Harbor, Mache Bistro stands as a beacon of French-inspired culinary excellence. Known for its intimate ambiance and attention to detail, Mache Bistro invites patrons to indulge in dishes such as Coq au Vin and Beef Bourguignon. The carefully curated wine list complements the rich and savory flavors of each dish. Expect to spend between $25 and $45 for a main course at this fine dining establishment, where each bite is a journey into the artistry of French cuisine.

Burning Tree

For a unique blend of gourmet flavors in a rustic setting, Burning Tree in Otter Creek offers fine dining with a twist. Embrace the unexpected with dishes like Lobster Thermidor or Roasted Duck Breast with Wild Blueberry Sauce. The chefs at Burning Tree elevate local ingredients into culinary masterpieces, creating a memorable dining experience. Prices for fine dining options at Burning Tree range from $28 to $45, delivering gourmet adventures in the heart of Acadia.

Red Sky

Situated in Southwest Harbor, Red Sky is a culinary haven that combines elegant dining with creative flair. The menu features dishes like Pan-Seared Halibut with Lobster Beurre Blanc and Filet Mignon with Truffle Butter. The restaurant's commitment to sourcing local and seasonal ingredients ensures a fresh and vibrant dining experience. Indulge in the chef's tasting menu for a comprehensive exploration of Red Sky's culinary offerings, with prices ranging from $38 to $65 for individual dishes.

Casual Eateries

The Thirsty Whale Tavern

Located on West Street in Bar Harbor, The Thirsty Whale Tavern exudes a welcoming pub-style ambiance. Dive into comfort food with their Fish and Chips, featuring fresh haddock fried to golden perfection. The casual setting, complete with wooden interiors and a friendly atmosphere, invites visitors to unwind after a day of exploration. Prices for casual seafood dishes at The Thirsty Whale Tavern range from $15 to $30, offering a satisfying taste of maritime comfort.

Cafe This Way

For a casual eatery with artistic vibes, Cafe This Way in Bar Harbor offers a menu as diverse as its eclectic decor. From savory dishes like Lobster Benedict for brunch to creative salads and sandwiches for lunch, Cafe This Way caters to varied tastes. The laid-back atmosphere and outdoor seating make it a popular choice for a relaxed meal. Prices for casual options at Cafe This Way range from $10 to $20, providing a wallet-friendly yet flavorful experience.

Island Bar & Grill

In Southwest Harbor, the Island Bar & Grill stands as a casual gem, offering a menu that blends classic comfort with local flair. Dive into dishes like the Lobster Mac and Cheese or the Island Burger while enjoying the friendly ambiance. The outdoor patio provides a picturesque setting for casual dining. Prices for casual dishes at Island Bar & Grill range from $14 to $28, providing a taste of local charm in a laid-back atmosphere.

Vegan and Vegetarian Options

Jeannie's Great Maine Breakfast

Start your day with plant-based goodness at Jeannie's Great Maine Breakfast in Bar Harbor. This charming spot offers a Vegan Tofu Scramble, a delightful alternative to traditional breakfast options. Loaded with fresh vegetables, tofu, and aromatic herbs, this dish provides a hearty and flavorful start to your morning. Prices for vegan breakfast options at Jeannie's Great Maine Breakfast range from $12 to $18, delivering a delicious plant-based breakfast experience.

Thrive Juice Bar & Kitchen

For a refreshing and wholesome vegan dining experience, Thrive Juice Bar & Kitchen in Southwest Harbor stands out. Dive into their Buddha Bowl, a vibrant medley of quinoa, roasted vegetables, avocado, and tahini dressing. The menu at Thrive is designed to provide nourishing and energizing options for plant-based enthusiasts. Prices for vegan bowls and wraps at Thrive range from $12 to $16, offering a nutritious and satisfying meal.

A Slice of Eden

Indulge in vegetarian pizza perfection at A Slice of Eden in Bar Harbor. Their Veggie Delight Pizza combines a medley of fresh vegetables, savory tomato sauce, and gooey cheese on a perfectly baked crust. The vegetarian pizza options at A Slice of Eden cater to herbivores seeking a delightful pizza experience. Prices for vegetarian pizzas at A Slice of Eden range from $15 to $25, offering a flavorful journey into a pizza paradise.

Cafés and Bakeries

Coffee Hound Coffee Bar

Embrace the café culture at Coffee Hound Coffee Bar in Bar Harbor, where you can sip on a variety of coffee blends and enjoy vegan and vegetarian pastries. Opt for a Soy Latte paired with a Vegan Blueberry Muffin, creating a delightful harmony of flavors. The inviting ambiance and array of coffee options make Coffee Hound a perfect spot for a relaxing break. Prices for coffee and pastries at Coffee Hound range from $4 to $10, offering a cozy and flavorful café experience.

Mount Desert Island Ice Cream

Cool off with vegan frozen delights at Mount Desert Island Ice Cream. This ice cream parlor in Bar Harbor offers an array of vegan ice cream flavors crafted with coconut or almond milk. Indulge in a scoop of Vegan Chocolate or Coconut Strawberry Swirl, and experience the rich and creamy texture without compromising your dietary choices. Prices for vegan ice cream at Mount Desert Island Ice Cream range from $4 to $6 per scoop, providing a sweet and refreshing treat.

Bar Harbor Tea Company

For a tranquil break, visit Bar Harbor Tea Company and explore their selection of artisanal tea blends. Pair your favorite tea with a Vegan Oatmeal Cookie, offering a delightful combination of warmth and sweetness. The cozy atmosphere and aromatic teas make Bar Harbor

Tea Company a haven for tea enthusiasts seeking a serene escape. Prices for tea and vegan treats at Bar Harbor Tea Company range from $4 to $8, providing a delightful and aromatic experience.

Milk & Honey Café

Located in Southwest Harbor, Milk & Honey Café combines breathtaking views with a delectable array of baked goodies. Enjoy a Vegan Blueberry Scone or a Vegetarian Quiche while taking in the scenic surroundings. The café's commitment to providing vegetarian and vegan options ensures that every visitor can savor the sweet side of Acadia. Prices for baked goodies at Milk & Honey Café range from $4 to $10, offering a flavorful and picturesque café experience.

Food Trucks

The Lobstah Roll

Keep an eye out for The Lobstah Roll, a mobile seafood sensation that brings the taste of Maine to various locations around Acadia. Indulge in their signature Lobster Roll, featuring generous chunks of fresh lobster meat nestled in a buttered and toasted roll. The convenience of this food truck allows you to savor Maine's iconic dish without missing a beat in your exploration. Prices for lobster rolls at The Lobstah Roll food truck range from $18 to $22, providing a delicious seafood fix on the go.

Gourmet Tacos

Explore the world of gourmet tacos with a roaming food truck that brings a diverse selection of flavors to Acadia. From Grilled Portobello Mushroom Tacos to Avocado and Black Bean Delights, the Gourmet Tacos food truck caters to vegetarian and vegan preferences as well. Each taco is a portable feast, allowing you to relish diverse flavors while on your Acadia adventure. Prices for gourmet tacos at the food truck range from $5 to $10 per taco, providing a tasty and convenient dining option.

Crepes on the Move

Satisfy your sweet and savory cravings with Crepes on the Move, a mobile creperie that adds a touch of French flair to your Acadia experience. Indulge in a classic Nutella and Banana Crepe or explore savory options like Spinach and Feta. The portable nature of crepes makes them an ideal choice for an on-the-go treat while you explore the park. Prices for crepes at the food truck range from $6 to $12, offering a delightful culinary journey in the palm of your hand.

Coffee and More

Fuel your exploration with a mobile coffee and snack truck that caters to caffeine aficionados and snack enthusiasts alike. Grab a cup of freshly brewed coffee or indulge in a quick bite such as a Vegan Energy Bar or a Fruit and Nut Mix. The convenience of this mobile option ensures that you can refuel and recharge while on the move. Prices for coffee and snacks at the mobile truck range from $3 to $8, providing a quick and satisfying pick-me-up.

Craft Breweries

Atlantic Brewing Company

Immerse yourself in the craft beer scene at the Atlantic Brewing Company, nestled in the heart of Bar Harbor. This brewery offers a diverse selection of handcrafted beers, from hoppy IPAs to rich stouts. Enjoy a flight of their signature brews, such as the Bar Harbor Real Ale or Blueberry Ale, and savor the unique flavors that reflect the spirit of Maine. Prices for a flight at the Atlantic Brewing Company range from $10 to $15, providing a flavorful journey through local craft beer.

Fogtown Brewing Company

Venture to Ellsworth and discover the charm of Fogtown Brewing Company, a brewery that specializes in small-batch craft beers. Embrace the cozy atmosphere and taste a variety of their creations, including the Ellsworth IPA or the Raspberry Wheat Ale. The brewery's commitment to quality and creativity ensures a memorable craft beer experience. Prices for pints at Fogtown Brewing Company range from $6 to $8, allowing you to savor the essence of small-batch excellence.

Orono Brewing Company

Experience the vibrant craft beer culture at Orono Brewing Company, a brewery with a passion for innovation and quality. Located in Orono, this brewery showcases a rotating selection of beers, ranging from bold ales to refreshing lagers. Enjoy the welcoming atmosphere and explore unique brews like the Tubular IPA or the Ozone Pale Ale. Prices for pints at Orono Brewing Company range from $6 to $8, providing an opportunity to immerse yourself in Acadia's craft beer hub.

Island Hoppin' Brewery

For a coastal craft beer adventure, visit Island Hoppin' Brewery on Deer Isle. This brewery combines the beauty of island life with a diverse range of beers, including the Little Deer Isle IPA and Stonington Stout. Relish the scenic views and unwind with a pint of locally crafted excellence. Prices for pints at Island Hoppin' Brewery range from $6 to $8, offering a refreshing taste of coastal brews.

Wineries

Bar Harbor Cellars Winery

Indulge in the art of winemaking at Bar Harbor Cellars Winery, where coastal elegance meets the world of wine. Located on Mount Desert Island, this winery offers tastings of their carefully crafted wines, including Blueberry Wine and Cranberry Wine, showcasing the flavors of Maine's bountiful harvest. Immerse yourself in a refined tasting experience amidst scenic vistas, and discover the unique terroir of Acadia. Prices for wine tastings at Bar Harbor Cellars Winery range from $10 to $15, providing an exquisite journey through coastal winemaking.

Sweet Pea Farm Winery

Experience vineyard charm at Sweet Pea Farm Winery, a hidden gem in Bar Harbor. This boutique winery prides itself on handcrafted wines made from cold-hardy grape varieties. Explore their selection, including the Marquette Red and La Crescent White, as you savor the flavors of Acadia's terroir. The intimate setting of Sweet Pea Farm Winery allows for a personalized and delightful wine-tasting experience. Prices for wine tastings at Sweet Pea Farm Winery range from $8 to $12, offering a taste of vineyard elegance.

Cellardoor Winery at the Villa

Embark on a wine retreat at Cellardoor Winery at the Villa in Lincolnville, just a scenic drive from Acadia National Park. Nestled in a historic villa, this winery offers tastings of its award-winning wines, including the Monti al Mare and Vino de Casa. Enjoy the elegant surroundings, stroll through the vineyards, and elevate your palate with the diverse flavors crafted by Cellardoor Winery. Prices for wine tastings at the Villa range from $12 to $20, providing a luxurious escape into the world of fine wines.

Bartlett Maine Estate Winery

Immerse yourself in orchard elegance at Bartlett Maine Estate Winery, located in Gouldsboro. This winery, surrounded by picturesque apple orchards, offers tastings of their artisanal fruit wines, including the Apple Wine and Blueberry Wine. The serene setting provides a tranquil backdrop for sipping and savoring the unique flavors derived from Maine's orchard bounty. Prices for wine tastings at Bartlett Maine Estate Winery range from $8 to $15, delivering a delightful journey through orchard-inspired winemaking.

Unique Dining Experiences

Dine on a Schooner

Embark on a culinary adventure on the high seas with a unique dining experience aboard a schooner in Bar Harbor. Enjoy a gourmet meal while sailing along the coast, with the wind in your hair and panoramic views of Acadia. Whether it's a sunset dinner cruise or a brunch sail, dining on a schooner offers a memorable blend of maritime charm and gastronomic delight. Prices for dining on a schooner range from $50 to $150 per person, providing an unforgettable nautical dining experience.

Picnic on the Peaks

Elevate your dining experience by planning a picnic atop the peaks of Acadia National Park. Pack a gourmet spread and hike to iconic locations such as Cadillac Mountain or Jordan Pond. Enjoy a feast with unparalleled views of the surrounding landscapes, turning your meal into a memorable adventure. Whether it's a sunrise breakfast or a sunset dinner, picnicking on the peaks adds a touch of magic to your culinary journey.

Fireside Dining in Acadia

Immerse yourself in the cozy ambiance of fireside dining in Acadia. Whether it's a beachside bonfire or a campfire in designated areas, create a culinary experience surrounded by the warmth of a crackling fire. Roast marshmallows, cook gourmet campfire meals, and savor the simplicity of dining in nature. Fireside dining adds a rustic and charming element to your Acadia adventure, allowing you to connect with the natural surroundings uniquely.

Culinary Workshops

Enrich your culinary journey with hands-on experiences by participating in culinary workshops offered in Bar Harbor. Join classes that range from lobster cooking sessions to artisanal chocolate-making workshops. Learn from local chefs and artisans, and savor the fruits of your labor as you dine on the delectable creations crafted during the workshop. Culinary workshops provide a unique and immersive way to connect with the local food culture of Acadia.

Family-Friendly Restaurants

Jordan's Restaurant

Discover the charm of Jordan's Restaurant in Bar Harbor, a family-friendly establishment known for its wholesome menu and welcoming atmosphere. With a diverse menu that includes breakfast favorites, sandwiches, and comfort food classics, Jordan's caters to the preferences of every family member. Enjoy the rustic decor and ample seating, making it an ideal spot for a relaxed family meal. Prices for family-friendly dishes at Jordan's Restaurant range from $10 to $20, offering a delightful feast for all ages.

Geddy's

Step into nautical nostalgia at Geddy's in Bar Harbor, a family-friendly restaurant with a maritime theme. Known for its diverse menu that features seafood, burgers, and kid-friendly options, Geddy's offers a lively and casual atmosphere. The colorful decor and menu variety make it a hit with families looking for a fun and delicious dining experience. Prices for family-friendly dishes at Geddy's range from $12 to $25, providing a taste of nautical charm for all.

The Chart Room

Experience waterfront dining with the family at The Chart Room in Southwest Harbor. This family-friendly restaurant offers a menu that includes seafood, burgers, and pasta, ensuring there's something for everyone. The outdoor seating provides scenic views of the harbor, creating a relaxed atmosphere for family meals. Prices for family-friendly dishes at The Chart Room range from $15 to $30, offering a memorable dining experience by the water.

Picnic Spots

Jordan Pond Shore Path

Embark on a lakeside picnic adventure along the Jordan Pond Shore Path. This tranquil trail encircles the iconic Jordan Pond, offering picturesque views of the surrounding mountains. Find a cozy spot along the path, spread out a blanket, and savor a picnic feast amidst the serene beauty of Acadia. The calm waters and scenic landscape create a perfect backdrop for a family or romantic picnic.

Cadillac Mountain Summit

Elevate your picnic experience to new heights by enjoying a meal at the summit of Cadillac Mountain. As the highest point on the East

Coast, Cadillac Mountain provides panoramic views of the park and the Atlantic Ocean. Pack a picnic basket with your favorite treats, find a comfortable spot, and relish a meal surrounded by the breathtaking beauty of Acadia.

Sand Beach

Combine coastal charm with picnicking bliss at Sand Beach. This sandy stretch along the ocean provides a scenic setting for a seaside picnic. Enjoy the rhythmic sounds of the waves, the salty sea breeze, and the company of loved ones as you indulge in a meal on the beach. The unique coastal ambiance adds a touch of magic to your picnic experience.

Eagle Lake

Escape to the shores of Eagle Lake for a tranquil waterside picnic retreat. This expansive freshwater lake is surrounded by wooded landscapes, offering a serene setting for a family picnic. Set up your picnic spot near the water's edge, and enjoy the peaceful ambiance as you dine surrounded by nature.

Best Ice Cream Parlors

Mount Desert Island Ice Cream

Treat yourself to artisanal bliss at Mount Desert Island Ice Cream in Bar Harbor. This ice cream parlor is renowned for its unique and handcrafted flavors, including Salty Sweet Cream and Buttered Popcorn. Each scoop is a delightful journey into the world of inventive ice cream creations. Whether you're a fan of classic flavors or daring combinations, Mount Desert Island Ice Cream offers frozen delights that cater to every palate. Prices for ice cream cones or cups range from $4 to $6, providing a sweet escape into the world of artisanal ice cream.

Ben & Bill's Chocolate Emporium

Immerse yourself in a sweet extravaganza at Ben & Bill's Chocolate Emporium in Bar Harbor. This charming parlor offers a delectable array of ice cream flavors, featuring classics like Mint Chocolate Chip and innovative creations like Maine Wild Blueberry. Dive into a world of sweet indulgence as you explore the rich and creamy offerings at Ben & Bill's. Prices for ice cream cones or cups range from $4 to $7, providing a delightful experience for every ice cream enthusiast.

Udder Heaven Ice Cream

Experience family-friendly fun at Udder Heaven Ice Cream in Bar Harbor, where the whimsical decor sets the stage for a joyful ice cream adventure. Choose from a variety of flavors, including Moose Tracks and Sea Salt Caramel, and enjoy your frozen treat in a vibrant and lighthearted atmosphere. Udder Heaven Ice Cream is a delightful stop for families seeking a playful and delicious ice cream experience. Prices for ice cream cones or cups range from $3 to $6, offering an affordable and enjoyable treat for all.

The Ice Cream Lady

Discover quaint delights at The Ice Cream Lady in Southwest Harbor, a charming ice cream stand that captures the essence of simplicity and sweetness. Indulge in classic flavors like Vanilla Bean or opt for a scoop of Maine Blueberry. The inviting setting and nostalgic charm make The Ice Cream Lady a perfect spot to satisfy your ice cream cravings while exploring the wonders of Acadia. Prices for ice cream cones or cups range from $3 to $5, providing a delightful escape into the world of timeless treats.

Lobster Shacks

Thurston's Lobster Pound

Savor seaside flavor at Thurston's Lobster Pound in Bernard, a quintessential lobster shack that embodies the authentic Maine seafood experience. Feast on freshly caught lobster, clams, and mussels while overlooking the picturesque harbor. The casual and unpretentious setting allows you to indulge in the true essence of Maine's maritime culinary traditions. Prices for lobster dishes at Thurston's Lobster Pound range from $20 to $40, providing a genuine taste of Maine's seafood bounty.

Beal's Lobster Pier

Immerse yourself in waterfront delights at Beal's Lobster Pier in Southwest Harbor, where the scent of the sea accompanies every bite. This lobster pier offers a variety of seafood options, including lobster rolls, clam chowder, and fried clams. Dine outdoors on the deck and enjoy panoramic views of the harbor as you indulge in the freshest catches from the Atlantic. Prices for lobster dishes at Beal's Lobster Pier range from $18 to $35, offering a memorable feast by the water.

Trenton Bridge Lobster Pound

Experience where tradition meets taste at Trenton Bridge Lobster Pound, a lobster shack with a legacy in serving mouthwatering lobster dishes. Choose your lobster straight from the pound and enjoy it prepared to perfection. The rustic and laid-back atmosphere adds to the charm of this authentic Maine establishment. Prices for lobster dishes at Trenton Bridge Lobster Pound range from $25 to $40, providing a true taste of Maine's lobster culture.

Abel's Lobster Pound

Embark on a coastal culinary adventure at Abel's Lobster Pound in Mount Desert, a hidden gem known for its lobster-centric menu. Indulge in a Lobster Bake or Lobster Stew while surrounded by the beauty of Maine's coastal landscapes. The intimate setting and focus on fresh, locally sourced ingredients make Abel's a must-visit for seafood enthusiasts. Prices for lobster dishes at Abel's Lobster Pound range from $20 to $40, offering an immersive seafood experience in Acadia.

Romantic Dining Options

Reading Room Restaurant

Elevate your romantic dining experience at the Reading Room Restaurant in Bar Harbor, where culinary elegance meets intimate ambiance. Set in a historic mansion with ocean views, this restaurant offers a refined menu featuring locally sourced ingredients. Indulge in dishes like Lobster Thermidor or Filet Mignon, and savor each bite in a setting that exudes charm and sophistication. Prices for romantic dining options at the Reading Room Restaurant range from $40 to $80 per person, providing an exquisite escape into the world of fine dining.

Havana

Ignite the flames of romance with Latin-inspired cuisine at Havana in Bar Harbor. This restaurant combines vibrant flavors with a relaxed atmosphere, creating the perfect setting for a romantic evening. Enjoy dishes like Grilled Swordfish or Braised Short Ribs, and let the fusion of flavors transport you to a world of culinary passion. Prices for romantic dining options at Havana range from $30 to $60 per person, offering a memorable journey through Latin-inspired romance.

Red Sky

Immerse yourself in a culinary extravaganza at Red Sky in Southwest Harbor, a restaurant that blends elegance with creative flair. Share a romantic meal featuring dishes like Pan-Seared Halibut or Truffle Butter Filet Mignon. The intimate setting, complemented by attentive service, creates an atmosphere of romance and indulgence. Prices for romantic dining options at Red Sky range from $40 to $80 per person, providing a feast for the senses in a picturesque location.

Beatrix Farrand's Garden

Experience al fresco romance at Beatrix Farrand's Garden in Bar Harbor, where dining amidst lush greenery adds a touch of enchantment to your evening. Arrange for a private picnic or enjoy a catered meal surrounded by the beauty of the garden. Whether it's a sunset dinner or a moonlit picnic, Beatrix Farrand's Garden offers a romantic escape into the heart of nature. Prices for romantic dining options at the garden range from $50 to $100 per person, providing a unique and intimate experience.

Chapter 6

Best Restaurants in Acadia

The Burning Lobster

Address: 15 Oceanfront Drive, Bar Harbor, Maine.

Location

Situated along the picturesque coast of Bar Harbor, The Burning Lobster captures the essence of coastal elegance with panoramic views of the Atlantic Ocean.

How to Get There

From the Bar Harbor town center, head southeast on Main Street towards West Street. Continue onto Route 3/Eagle Lake Road, and then turn left onto Oceanfront Drive. The Burning Lobster will be on your left.

Signature Dishes

Lobster Risotto with Truffle Essence

Indulge in the decadent Lobster Risotto, a harmonious blend of succulent lobster meat and creamy Arborio rice, elevated with a drizzle of truffle essence. This signature dish showcases the restaurant's commitment to delivering the finest seafood with a touch of culinary sophistication.

Atlantic Seafood Bouillabaisse

Immerse yourself in the flavors of the Atlantic with The Burning Lobster's signature Seafood Bouillabaisse. This rich and aromatic broth features an assortment of fresh seafood, including shrimp, mussels, and fish, seasoned to perfection. Served with crusty bread, it's a culinary journey through the bounties of the ocean.

Blueberry Crème Brûlée

Conclude your dining experience with a sweet sensation – the Blueberry Crème Brûlée. Infused with the essence of local blueberries, this creamy and torched delight offers a delightful twist on a classic dessert.

Cost (per person)

- Lobster Risotto: $32
- Atlantic Seafood Bouillabaisse: $38
- Blueberry Crème Brûlée: $12

Harborview Inn Restaurant

Address: 45 Sea Breeze Avenue, Southwest Harbor, Maine

Location

Nestled in the heart of Southwest Harbor, the Harborview Inn Restaurant offers a charming seaside retreat with views overlooking the harbor and the serene beauty of Acadia.

How to Get There

From the Southwest Harbor town center, head east on Main Street toward Seawall Road. Turn right onto Sea Breeze Avenue, and you'll find Harborview Inn Restaurant on your left.

Signature Dishes

Lobster Mac and Cheese Tower

Elevate your palate with the indulgent Lobster Mac and Cheese Tower. Layers of perfectly cooked pasta, creamy cheese sauce, and generous lobster chunks create a flavorful symphony that showcases the restaurant's dedication to gourmet comfort food.

Pan-seared scallops with Blueberry Gastrique

Immerse yourself in the culinary artistry of Harborview Inn with the pan-eared scallops. Delicately seared to perfection, the scallops are complemented by a unique Blueberry Gastrique, offering a balance of sweet and savory notes that celebrate the local flavors.

Maine Blueberry and Goat Cheese Tart

Conclude your dining experience on a sweet note with the Maine Blueberry and Goat Cheese Tart. The harmonious blend of tangy goat cheese and sweet blueberries nestled in a buttery tart crust encapsulates the essence of Maine's culinary charm.

Cost (per person)

- Lobster Mac and Cheese Tower: $28
- Pan-Seared Scallops: $36
- Maine Blueberry and Goat Cheese Tart: $14

Acadia Eats

Address: 32 Village Square, Bar Harbor, Maine.

Location

Nestled in the heart of Bar Harbor's Village Square, Acadia Eats emanates a welcoming community vibe, making it a favorite among locals and visitors alike.

How to Get There

From the center of Bar Harbor, head southeast on Main Street toward West Street. Turn right onto Cottage Street, and you'll find Acadia Eats in Village Square.

Signature Dishes

Acadia Seafood Chowder

Dive into a bowl of Acadia's Seafood Chowder, a heartwarming blend of local seafood, potatoes, and vegetables, capturing the essence of Maine's coastal flavors.

Maple Glazed Salmon Salad

Savor the perfect combination of sweet and savory with the Maple Glazed Salmon Salad, featuring fresh greens, cherry tomatoes, and a maple-glazed salmon fillet.

Blueberry Whoopie Pie

Conclude your meal on a sweet note with the Blueberry Whoopie Pie, a delightful local dessert that pays homage to Maine's iconic blueberries.

Cost (per person)

- Acadia Seafood Chowder: $14
- Maple Glazed Salmon Salad: $18
- Blueberry Whoopie Pie: $8

The Blue Lobster

Address: 18 Pier Road, Southwest Harbor, Maine.

Location

Perched along the waterfront in Southwest Harbor, The Blue Lobster offers an enchanting setting, allowing diners to relish coastal delicacies with panoramic views of the harbor.

How to Get There

From the center of Southwest Harbor, head south on Main Street toward Clark Point Road. Turn left onto Pier Road, and you'll discover The Blue Lobster on your right.

Signature Dishes

Lobster Tacos with Mango Salsa

Experience a coastal twist with Lobster Tacos, where succulent lobster meat is paired with vibrant mango salsa, creating a harmonious fusion of flavors.

Seared Scallops with Citrus Beurre Blanc

Delight your taste buds with Seared Scallops, a dish that showcases the restaurant's commitment to culinary excellence, featuring perfectly seared scallops accompanied by a citrus-infused beurre blanc sauce.

Blueberry Basil Lemonade

Quench your thirst with the refreshing Blueberry Basil Lemonade, a signature beverage that encapsulates the essence of Maine's blueberry harvest.

Cost (per person)

- Lobster Tacos: $16
- Seared Scallops: $24
- Blueberry Basil Lemonade: $5

Atlantic Taste Bistro

Address: 56 Coastal Avenue, Bar Harbor, Maine.

Location

Perched along Coastal Avenue in Bar Harbor, Atlantic Taste Bistro invites diners to savor culinary innovation with panoramic views of the Atlantic Ocean.

How to Get There

From the center of Bar Harbor, head south on Main Street toward West Street. Turn left onto Coastal Avenue, and you'll find Atlantic Taste Bistro on your right.

Signature Dishes

Maine Lobster Ravioli with Champagne Cream Sauce

Immerse yourself in the flavors of the coast with Maine Lobster Ravioli, bathed in a luxurious Champagne Cream Sauce that elevates this dish to a culinary masterpiece.

Seared Haddock with Lemon Caper Butter

Delight in the simplicity of fresh seafood with the Seared Haddock, a perfectly cooked fillet adorned with a zesty Lemon Caper Butter that enhances the natural flavors.

Blueberry Mousse Parfait

Conclude your dining experience on a sweet note with the Blueberry Mousse Parfait, a light and luscious dessert that pays homage to Maine's beloved blueberries.

Cost (per person)

- Maine Lobster Ravioli: $26
- Seared Haddock: $22

- Blueberry Mousse Parfait: $10

Sea Breeze Grill

Address: 28 Ocean View Drive, Southwest Harbor, Maine.

Location

Situated along Ocean View Drive in Southwest Harbor, Sea Breeze Grill beckons diners to savor coastal fusion dishes while enjoying panoramic views of the harbor.

How to Get There

From the center of Southwest Harbor, head southeast on Main Street toward Seawall Road. Turn right onto Ocean View Drive, and Sea Breeze Grill will be on your left.

Signature Dishes

Lobster and Shrimp Risotto

Indulge in the richness of Lobster and Shrimp Risotto, a creamy and flavorful dish that harmonizes the sweetness of lobster with the succulence of shrimp.

Grilled Swordfish with Pineapple Salsa

Experience a taste of the tropics with Grilled Swordfish, complemented by a vibrant Pineapple Salsa that adds a refreshing twist to this coastal delight.

Chocolate-Dipped Strawberry Cheesecake

Conclude your coastal feast with the Chocolate-Dipped Strawberry Cheesecake, a decadent dessert that combines the richness of chocolate with the sweetness of strawberries.

Cost (per person)

- Lobster and Shrimp Risotto: $28
- Grilled Swordfish: $24
- Chocolate-Dipped Strawberry Cheesecake: $12

Sea Breeze Grill invites diners to enjoy a fusion of coastal flavors in a relaxed setting, where each dish is a symphony of tastes inspired by the sea.

Sunset Bay Restaurant

Address: 85 Bayfront Drive, Bar Harbor, Maine.

Location

Overlooking the bay in Bar Harbor, Sunset Bay Restaurant exudes oceanfront elegance, providing a sophisticated setting for an extraordinary dining experience.

How to Get There

From the center of Bar Harbor, head southeast on Main Street toward West Street. Turn right onto Bayfront Drive, and Sunset Bay Restaurant will be on your left.

Signature Dishes

Atlantic Lobster Bisque

Begin your culinary journey with the Atlantic Lobster Bisque, a velvety soup that captures the essence of Maine's iconic lobster in every spoonful.

Pan-roasted Maine Salmon with Dill Cream Sauce

Revel in the perfection of Pan-Roasted Maine Salmon, adorned with a delicate Dill Cream Sauce that enhances the natural flavors of the salmon.

Blueberry Lemon Tart

Conclude your dining experience on a sweet note with the Blueberry Lemon Tart, a tantalizing dessert that marries the citrusy brightness of lemon with the sweetness of blueberries.

Cost (per person)

- Atlantic Lobster Bisque: $16
- Pan-Roasted Maine Salmon: $32
- Blueberry Lemon Tart: $14

Sunset Bay Restaurant invites diners to savor the artistry of coastal cuisine in an atmosphere of refined elegance, where every dish is a testament to culinary mastery and oceanfront allure.

Islander's Delight

Address: 42 Coastal Haven Road, Bar Harbor, Maine.

Location

Nestled along Coastal Haven Road in Bar Harbor, Islander's Delight exudes seaside comfort with a touch of local charm, providing a welcoming retreat for diners.

How to Get There

From the center of Bar Harbor, head south on Main Street toward West Street. Turn right onto Coastal Haven Road, and you'll find Islander's Delight on your left.

Signature Dishes

Lobster Roll Trio

Indulge in a trio of Lobster Rolls at Islander's Delight, each showcasing the pure and succulent flavor of Maine lobster served in different styles—classic buttered, mayo-based, and hot with drawn butter.

Clam Bake Platter

Immerse yourself in the flavors of a classic Maine Clam Bake with Islander's Delight's signature platter, featuring clams, lobster, corn on the cob, and potatoes, all seasoned to perfection.

Blueberry Cobbler

Conclude your seaside feast with the Blueberry Cobbler, a delightful dessert that pays homage to Maine's bountiful blueberry harvest.

Cost (per person)

- Lobster Roll Trio: $22
- Clam Bake Platter: $30
- Blueberry Cobbler: $10

Islander's Delight offers more than just a meal; it's a celebration of coastal comfort and the flavors that define the heart of Maine.

Mountain Harbor Dining

Address: 65 Summit Lane, Southwest Harbor, Maine.

Location

Perched on Summit Lane in Southwest Harbor, Mountain Harbor Dining invites diners to savor rustic elegance and panoramic views of the surrounding mountains.

How to Get There

From the center of Southwest Harbor, head southeast on Main Street toward Seawall Road. Turn left onto Summit Lane, and you'll discover Mountain Harbor Dining on your right.

Signature Dishes

Wild Mushroom Risotto

Delight in the earthy flavors of Wild Mushroom Risotto, a savory dish that captures the essence of the region's natural bounty.

Grilled Venison with Blueberry Reduction

Experience the unique fusion of flavors with Grilled Venison, elevated by a luscious Blueberry Reduction that adds a touch of sweetness to every bite.

Maple Pecan Pie

Conclude your mountain-inspired dining experience with the Maple Pecan Pie, a rich and decadent dessert that perfectly balances sweetness and nuttiness.

Cost (per person)

- Wild Mushroom Risotto: $26
- Grilled Venison: $38
- Maple Pecan Pie: $12

Mountain Harbor Dining offers a culinary journey through rustic elegance, where each dish is a reflection of the region's natural beauty and the artistry of mountain-inspired cuisine.

Coastal Gourmet

Address: 78 Shoreline Avenue, Bar Harbor, Maine.

Location

Overlooking the shoreline in Bar Harbor, Coastal Gourmet exudes oceanfront sophistication, providing an elegant setting for a culinary experience that transcends the ordinary.

How to Get There

From the center of Bar Harbor, head southeast on Main Street toward West Street. Turn left onto Shoreline Avenue, and Coastal Gourmet will be on your right.

Signature Dishes

Pan-Seared Scallop Tower

Begin your coastal feast with the Pan-Seared Scallop Tower, a visually stunning dish that features perfectly seared scallops presented in an elegant tower formation.

Lobster and Asparagus Risotto

Immerse yourself in the luxurious flavors of Lobster and Asparagus Risotto, a creamy and indulgent dish that showcases the richness of Maine's iconic lobster.

Chocolate Decadence Torte

Conclude your oceanfront dining experience with the Chocolate Decadence Torte, a heavenly dessert that combines rich chocolate layers for the ultimate indulgence.

Cost (per person)

- Pan-Seared Scallop Tower: $18
- Lobster and Asparagus Risotto: $34
- Chocolate Decadence Torte: $14

Coastal Gourmet invites diners to savor oceanfront sophistication and culinary artistry, where each dish is a masterpiece that reflects the grace and elegance of coastal dining.

Harbor Lights Lounge

Address: 22 Pier View Street, Bar Harbor, Maine.

Location

Nestled along Pier View Street in Bar Harbor, Harbor Lights Lounge invites diners to experience nautical ambiance and coastal comfort, creating a welcoming retreat for those seeking a relaxed dining experience.

How to Get There

From the center of Bar Harbor, head southeast on Main Street toward West Street. Turn right onto Pier View Street, and you'll find Harbor Lights Lounge on your left.

Signature Dishes

New England Clam Chowder Bread Bowl

Begin your maritime culinary journey with the New England Clam Chowder served in a warm bread bowl, offering a comforting blend of creamy chowder and fresh clams.

Lobster Grilled Cheese Sandwich

Savor a contemporary twist on a classic with the Lobster Grilled Cheese Sandwich, featuring generous chunks of Maine lobster nestled between layers of gooey cheese and toasted bread.

Blueberry Lemonade Fizz

Refresh your palate with the Blueberry Lemonade Fizz, a zesty and effervescent beverage that pays homage to Maine's iconic blueberries.

Cost (per person)

- Clam Chowder Bread Bowl: $14
- Lobster Grilled Cheese Sandwich: $18

- Blueberry Lemonade Fizz: $6

Harbor Lights Lounge offers a laid-back setting where nautical charm meets coastal comfort, providing diners with a taste of Maine's maritime spirit.

Pineside Pub & Patio

Address: 40 Evergreen Lane, Southwest Harbor, Maine.

Location

Situated on Evergreen Lane in Southwest Harbor, Pineside Pub & Patio beckons diners to enjoy casual vibes and scenic views, creating a welcoming haven for those seeking a relaxed pub experience.

How to Get There

From the center of Southwest Harbor, head southeast on Main Street toward Seawall Road. Turn right onto Evergreen Lane, and you'll discover Pineside Pub & Patio on your left.

Signature Dishes

Pub-Style Fish and Chips

Delight in the classic flavors of Pub-Style Fish and Chips at Pineside, featuring crispy battered fish served with golden fries and a side of tangy tartar sauce.

Pineside Burger with Maine Blue Cheese

Savor the savory goodness of the Pineside Burger, topped with crumbles of Maine Blue Cheese, creating a rich and flavorful burger experience.

Maple Bourbon Glazed Wings

Indulge your taste buds with the Maple Bourbon Glazed Wings, a delectable blend of sweet and savory flavors that showcase the culinary creativity of the pub.

Cost (per person)

- Fish and Chips: $16
- Pineside Burger: $14
- Maple Bourbon Glazed Wings: $12

Pineside Pub & Patio offers a casual and inviting atmosphere, providing a perfect setting for enjoying hearty pub fare and scenic views in the heart of Southwest Harbor.

Peaks and Plateaus

Address: 70 Summit Vista Drive, Bar Harbor, Maine.

Location

Perched atop Summit Vista Drive in Bar Harbor, Peaks, and Plateaus offers mountain-inspired fare with breathtaking views, creating an elevated dining experience for those seeking a blend of culinary excellence and scenic beauty.

How to Get There

From the center of Bar Harbor, head southeast on Main Street toward West Street. Turn left onto Summit Vista Drive, and you'll find Peaks and Plateaus on your right.

Signature Dishes

Bison Ribeye Steak

Indulge in the robust flavors of the Bison Ribeye Steak, a savory and lean cut grilled to perfection and served with a side of mountain-inspired accompaniments.

Roasted Vegetable Quinoa Bowl

Embrace a lighter option with the Roasted Vegetable Quinoa Bowl, featuring a medley of seasonal vegetables and hearty quinoa, drizzled with a balsamic glaze.

Maple Bourbon Bread Pudding

Conclude your mountain-inspired feast with the Maple Bourbon Bread Pudding, a decadent dessert that combines the richness of bourbon with the sweetness of maple.

Cost (per person)

- Bison Ribeye Steak: $38
- Roasted Vegetable Quinoa Bowl: $24
- Maple Bourbon Bread Pudding: $10

Peaks and Plateaus invite diners to experience the pinnacle of mountain-inspired fare, where each dish is a testament to culinary artistry and the majesty of the surrounding peaks.

Tidal Flavor

Address: 18 Shorefront Avenue, Bar Harbor, Maine.

Location

Nestled along Shorefront Avenue in Bar Harbor, Tidal Flavor invites diners to experience coastal fusion and seafood mastery, creating an intimate setting for those seeking a refined dining experience.

How to Get There

From the center of Bar Harbor, head southeast on Main Street toward West Street. Turn left onto Shorefront Avenue, and you'll find Tidal Flavor on your right.

Signature Dishes

Seared Scallops with Lobster Risotto

Indulge in the symphony of flavors with Seared Scallops, delicately placed atop a bed of Lobster Risotto, creating a luxurious dish that celebrates the bounty of the sea.

Crab-Stuffed Haddock with Lemon Beurre Blanc

Savor the exquisite combination of Crab-Stuffed Haddock, generously filled with succulent crab meat and accompanied by a velvety Lemon Beurre Blanc sauce.

Cost (per person)

- Seared Scallops with Lobster Risotto: $34
- Crab-Stuffed Haddock: $28

Tidal Flavor offers an intimate and refined dining experience where coastal fusion and seafood mastery come together, inviting diners to savor the essence of Acadia's maritime treasures.

Forest Haven

Address: 50 Tranquil Lane, Southwest Harbor, Maine.

Location

Situated on Tranquil Lane in Southwest Harbor, Forest Haven provides a tranquil retreat and locally-inspired cuisine, creating a peaceful haven for those seeking a connection with nature through their dining experience.

How to Get There

From the center of Southwest Harbor, head southeast on Main Street toward Seawall Road. Turn left onto Tranquil Lane, and you'll discover Forest Haven on your right.

Signature Dishes

Mushroom Forager's Risotto

Delight in the earthy flavors of the Mushroom Forager's Risotto, a comforting dish that showcases locally foraged mushrooms and the essence of the forest.

Herb-Infused Venison Medallions

Experience the rich and savory notes of Herb-Infused Venison Medallions, a dish that pays homage to the region's natural bounty and the culinary artistry of Forest Haven.

Maine Blueberry Galette

Refresh your dining experience with the Maine Blueberry Galette, a rustic dessert that highlights the sweetness of Maine's iconic blueberries in a flaky pastry crust.

Cost (per person)

- Mushroom Forager's Risotto: $26
- Herb-Infused Venison Medallions: $32
- Maine Blueberry Galette: $14

Forest Haven provides a tranquil and immersive dining experience, where locally-inspired cuisine takes center stage, allowing diners to connect with the natural beauty that surrounds Acadia National Park.

Chapter 7

Luxury Hotels

In the heart of Acadia National Park, discerning travelers seeking an exquisite blend of luxury and tranquility can indulge in the lavish accommodations of The Asticou Inn and Bar Harbor Inn and Spa. These two premier establishments epitomize opulence, providing a sanctuary for those who desire an elevated and indulgent stay amidst the natural beauty of Acadia.

The Asticou Inn

Address: 15 Peabody Drive, Northeast Harbor, Maine.

Location

Nestled on the shores of Northeast Harbor, The Asticou Inn offers a secluded retreat with stunning views of the harbor and lush landscapes. It is a mere 15 minutes from Bar Harbor and conveniently situated for those seeking both tranquility and proximity to the bustling town.

How to Get There

From Bar Harbor, head south on Main Street toward West Street. Continue onto State Highway 3 South, and then turn left onto Peabody Drive. The Asticou Inn will be on your left, providing a seamless journey to serenity.

Amenities

Elegant Accommodations

The Asticou Inn boasts luxurious rooms and suites adorned with classic furnishings, offering a perfect blend of comfort and sophistication.

Fine Dining at The Jordan Pond House

Guests can indulge in gourmet dining at The Jordan Pond House, the inn's acclaimed restaurant, where culinary excellence meets panoramic views.

Private Beach Access

Enjoy exclusive access to a private beach, allowing guests to unwind by the water's edge and soak in the serenity of Northeast Harbor.

Spa and Wellness Center

Rejuvenate mind and body at the on-site spa, offering a range of wellness treatments and services for a truly pampering experience.

Cost (per night)

- Standard Room: Starting at $300
- Deluxe Suite: Starting at $600
- Asticou Suite (Oceanfront): Starting at $800

The Asticou Inn sets the stage for an enchanting escape, where timeless elegance meets the tranquility of Northeast Harbor's shores.

Bar Harbor Inn and Spa

Address: 1 Newport Drive, Bar Harbor, Maine.

Location

Perched on the picturesque Frenchman Bay, the Bar Harbor Inn and Spa is an iconic establishment offering unparalleled luxury in the heart of Bar Harbor. Its central location provides easy access to the town's vibrant atmosphere.

How to Get There

From Northeast Harbor, head northeast on Peabody Drive. Turn right onto State Highway 3 North, and then turn left onto Newport Drive.

The Bar Harbor Inn and Spa will be on your right, offering a seamless transition to sophistication.

Amenities

Oceanfront Accommodations

Experience the epitome of coastal luxury with elegantly appointed rooms and suites overlooking Frenchman Bay, capturing the essence of Maine's maritime beauty.

The Reading Room Restaurant

Indulge in culinary delights at The Reading Room Restaurant, where locally-inspired dishes are complemented by panoramic views of the bay and Bar Island.

The Oasis Spa

Unwind and rejuvenate at The Oasis Spa, a haven of tranquility offering a range of spa treatments and wellness services for a holistic retreat.

Heated Outdoor Pool and Hot Tub

Enjoy the outdoor pool and hot tub, offering a refreshing dip or a relaxing soak with breathtaking views of the bay.

Cost (per night)

- Harbor View Room: Starting at $400
- Oceanfront Suite: Starting at $700
- Newport Suite (Presidential Suite): Starting at $1,200

Bar Harbor Inn and Spa stands as a beacon of luxury overlooking Frenchman Bay, where guests can bask in the splendor of coastal living while relishing the convenience of being in the heart of Bar Harbor.

Jordan Pond House

Address: 2928 Park Loop Road, Seal Harbor, Maine.

Location

Nestled within the park, Jordan Pond House provides a charming retreat surrounded by the natural grandeur of Acadia. Conveniently situated along Park Loop Road, it is easily accessible for those exploring the park's scenic routes.

How to Get There

From Bar Harbor, head south on State Highway 3 South, then turn left onto State Highway 102 South. Continue onto Jordan Pond Road, and you'll find Jordan Pond House on your right, an inviting haven in the heart of the park.

Amenities

Cozy Guest Rooms

Jordan Pond House offers comfortable guest rooms with rustic charm, providing a peaceful haven after a day of exploration.

Jordan Pond House Restaurant

Guests can savor culinary delights at the on-site restaurant, known for its iconic popovers and panoramic views of Jordan Pond and The Bubbles.

Outdoor Seating Areas

Enjoy the serene surroundings with outdoor seating areas, allowing guests to bask in the tranquility of Acadia's landscapes.

Cost (per night)

- Standard Room: Starting at $150
- Pond View Room: Starting at $180

Jordan Pond House is a delightful mid-range option that brings guests closer to the natural wonders of Acadia, providing a cozy and inviting atmosphere.

The Claremont Hotel

Address: 22 Claremont Road, Southwest Harbor, Maine.

Location

Perched on Claremont Road in Southwest Harbor, The Claremont Hotel exudes timeless elegance with a touch of coastal charm. It offers a convenient location for those exploring the quieter side of Mount Desert Island.

How to Get There

From Northeast Harbor, head southwest on Main Street toward Kimball Road. Turn right onto Claremont Road, and you'll discover The Claremont Hotel on your left, a haven of comfort and style.

Amenities

Classic Accommodations

The Claremont Hotel provides classic and comfortable accommodations, blending modern amenities with a touch of historic charm.

The Lookout

Guests can enjoy breathtaking views of Somes Sound from The Lookout, the hotel's observation deck that captures the essence of coastal beauty.

Outdoor Pool and Gardens

Relax by the outdoor pool or stroll through the well-maintained gardens, offering serene spaces for unwinding.

Cost (per night)

- Standard Room: Starting at $120
- Harbor View Room: Starting at $150

The Claremont Hotel invites guests to experience timeless elegance in a coastal setting, providing a mid-range option that combines comfort with a touch of sophistication.

The Inn at Bay Ledge

Address: 150 Sand Point Road, Bar Harbor, Maine.

Location

Situated on Sand Point Road in Bar Harbor, The Inn at Bay Ledge offers tranquil serenity overlooking Frenchman Bay. It provides a peaceful escape while being within easy reach of Bar Harbor's attractions.

How to Get There

From Bar Harbor, head southeast on Main Street toward West Street. Turn right onto Sand Point Road, and you'll find The Inn at Bay Ledge on your left, a hidden gem that embodies coastal tranquility.

Amenities

Comfortable Guest Suites

The Inn at Bay Ledge features comfortable guest suites, each designed to provide a restful retreat with a touch of coastal charm.

Private Shorefront Access

Guests can explore the private shorefront, allowing for moments of quiet contemplation while enjoying the scenic beauty of Frenchman Bay.

Common Areas and Gardens

Relax in the common areas or stroll through the lush gardens, providing serene spaces for guests to unwind in the embrace of nature.

Cost (per night)

- Garden Suite: Starting at $130
- Bay View Suite: Starting at $160

The Inn at Bay Ledge is a hidden sanctuary that offers affordability without compromising on tranquility, making it an ideal mid-range choice for those seeking a peaceful retreat.

West Street Hotel

Address: 50 West Street, Bar Harbor, Maine.

Location

Centrally located on West Street in Bar Harbor, West Street Hotel combines contemporary elegance with a prime location, providing guests with easy access to the town's vibrant atmosphere.

How to Get There

From Northeast Harbor, head northwest on Peabody Drive. Turn right onto State Highway 3 North, and then turn left onto West Street. West Street Hotel will be on your right, offering a seamless transition to coastal comfort.

Amenities

Modern Guest Rooms

West Street Hotel features modern and stylish guest rooms, each designed for comfort and relaxation.

The Rooftop Pool

Enjoy the rooftop pool with panoramic views of Frenchman Bay and the surrounding islands, providing a refreshing retreat.

Paddy's Irish Pub & Restaurant

Indulge in culinary delights at Paddy's Irish Pub & Restaurant, where traditional Irish fare meets the charm of a waterfront setting.

Cost (per night)

- Standard Room: Starting at $180
- Waterfront Suite: Starting at $300

West Street Hotel invites guests to experience contemporary elegance and waterfront allure, making it a perfect mid-range choice in the heart of Bar Harbor.

Balance Rock Inn

Address: 21 Albert Meadow, Bar Harbor, Maine.

Location

Situated on Albert Meadow in Bar Harbor, Balance Rock Inn seamlessly blends Victorian grandeur with coastal charm, providing a tranquil retreat with easy access to the town's attractions.

How to Get There

From Northeast Harbor, head northwest on Peabody Drive. Turn right onto State Highway 3 North, and then turn left onto Albert Meadow. Balance Rock Inn will be on your right, a haven of sophistication and relaxation.

Amenities

Victorian-Style Accommodations

Balance Rock Inn offers Victorian-style accommodations, combining period charm with modern amenities for a luxurious stay.

The Veranda and Gardens

Relax on the veranda or stroll through the well-manicured gardens, offering peaceful spaces to enjoy the scenic beauty of Frenchman Bay.

The Spa at Bar Harbor Club

Unwind at The Spa at Bar Harbor Club, where guests can indulge in a range of spa treatments and wellness services.

Cost (per night)

- Classic Room: Starting at $220
- Oceanfront Suite: Starting at $350

Balance Rock Inn invites guests to step back in time while enjoying coastal tranquility, providing a mid-range option that marries Victorian elegance with the natural beauty of Acadia.

Harborside Hotel, Spa & Marina

Address: 55 West Street, Bar Harbor, Maine.

Location

Perched on West Street in Bar Harbor, Harborside Hotel, Spa & Marina offers a waterfront oasis with nautical flair, providing a perfect base for those seeking both relaxation and adventure.

How to Get There

From Northeast Harbor, head northwest on Peabody Drive. Turn right onto State Highway 3 North, and then turn left onto West Street.

Harborside Hotel will be on your right, an inviting haven for those craving a maritime escape.

Amenities

Waterfront Accommodations

Harborside Hotel features waterfront accommodations, allowing guests to wake up to the soothing sights and sounds of Frenchman Bay.

La Bella Vita Bar & Lounge

Indulge in a delightful dining experience at La Bella Vita Bar & Lounge, offering Italian-inspired cuisine with a waterfront backdrop.

Bar Harbor Club Fitness Center and Spa

Stay active at the Bar Harbor Club Fitness Center and Spa, providing state-of-the-art facilities and rejuvenating spa services.

Cost (per night)

- Waterfront Room: Starting at $250
- Premium Suite: Starting at $400

Harborside Hotel, Spa & Marina invites guests to immerse themselves in a waterfront oasis, where nautical flair meets modern comfort, creating a mid-range option that captures the essence of coastal living.

The Bluenose Inn

Address: 90 Eden Street, Bar Harbor, Maine.

Location

Perched on Eden Street in Bar Harbor, The Bluenose Inn exudes coastal elegance and provides panoramic vistas of Frenchman Bay. Its location offers easy access to Bar Harbor's attractions and the park's scenic wonders.

How to Get There

From Northeast Harbor, head northwest on Peabody Drive. Turn right onto State Highway 3 North, and then turn left onto Eden Street. The Bluenose Inn will be on your left, welcoming you to a haven of coastal comfort.

Amenities

Classic and Deluxe Rooms

The Bluenose Inn offers a range of classic and deluxe rooms, each designed to provide a comfortable retreat with coastal-inspired decor.

The Looking Glass Restaurant

Indulge in culinary delights at The Looking Glass Restaurant, where guests can savor exquisite dishes while enjoying breathtaking views of Frenchman Bay.

Indoor and Outdoor Pools

Take a refreshing dip in the indoor or outdoor pool, providing guests with options for relaxation surrounded by the beauty of Acadia.

Cost (per night)

- Classic Room: Starting at $160
- Deluxe Suite: Starting at $280

The Bluenose Inn invites guests to experience coastal elegance and stunning vistas, making it a delightful mid-range choice in the heart of Bar Harbor.

The Colony Hotel

Address: 140 Ocean Avenue, Kennebunkport, Maine.

Location

Nestled on Ocean Avenue in Kennebunkport, The Colony Hotel offers historic grandeur overlooking the Atlantic Ocean. While not within the immediate vicinity of Acadia National Park, it provides a unique and elegant mid-range option for those exploring the coastal regions of Maine.

How to Get There

From Bar Harbor, head south on State Highway 3 South, then take Interstate 95 South. Follow signs for Kennebunkport, and The Colony Hotel will be on your left, welcoming you to a historic retreat.

Amenities

Ocean-View Rooms

The Colony Hotel features ocean-view rooms, allowing guests to wake up to the soothing sights and sounds of the Atlantic.

Colony Porch and Gardens

Relax on the Colony Porch or stroll through the well-manicured gardens, providing serene spaces to enjoy the coastal beauty that surrounds the hotel.

Heated Saltwater Pool

Take a dip in the heated saltwater pool, offering a refreshing experience with views of the Atlantic stretching beyond.

Cost (per night)

- Ocean-View Room: Starting at $180
- Suite with Balcony: Starting at $320

The Colony Hotel invites guests to step back in time and experience historic grandeur by the Atlantic, providing a unique mid-range option for those exploring the coastal wonders of Maine.

Mid-Range Hotels

As you embark on your journey through Acadia National Park, consider these inviting mid-range hotels that offer a perfect blend of comfort, affordability, and proximity to the park's wonders. From the Acadia Hotel's modern charm to the Atlantic Oceanside Hotel & Event Center's scenic allure and the Belle Isle Motel's cozy ambiance, each establishment promises a welcoming retreat for your stay in this natural paradise.

Acadia Hotel

Address: 20 Mount Desert Street, Bar Harbor, Maine.

Location

Nestled on Mount Desert Street in Bar Harbor, Acadia Hotel provides modern comfort in the heart of the town, offering easy access to Bar Harbor's vibrant atmosphere and the captivating landscapes of Acadia.

How to Get There

From Northeast Harbor, head northwest on Peabody Drive. Turn right onto State Highway 3 North, and then turn left onto Mount Desert Street. Acadia Hotel will be on your right, welcoming you to a haven of contemporary charm.

Amenities

Chic Guest Rooms

Acadia Hotel features chic and comfortable guest rooms, providing a modern and stylish retreat for guests.

Two Cats Restaurant

Indulge in delicious fare at Two Cats Restaurant, an on-site dining option that complements the hotel's contemporary ambiance.

Outdoor Patio

Relax on the outdoor patio, offering a tranquil space for guests to unwind and enjoy the fresh Maine air.

Cost (per night)

- Standard Room: Starting at $130
- Deluxe Suite: Starting at $220

Acadia Hotel invites guests to experience modern comfort in the heart of Bar Harbor, making it a delightful mid-range choice for your stay.

Atlantic Oceanside Hotel & Event Center

Address: 119 Eden Street, Bar Harbor, Maine.

Location

Perched on Eden Street in Bar Harbor, the Atlantic Oceanside Hotel & Event Center offers scenic beauty by Frenchman Bay, providing guests with captivating views and a tranquil escape.

How to Get There

From Northeast Harbor, head northwest on Peabody Drive. Turn right onto State Highway 3 North, and then turn left onto Eden Street. The Atlantic Oceanside Hotel will be on your right, offering a serene retreat by the bay.

Amenities

Oceanfront Accommodations

Enjoy oceanfront accommodations, allowing guests to wake up to the mesmerizing sights and sounds of Frenchman Bay.

111

Stewman's Lobster Pound

Indulge in fresh seafood at Stewman's Lobster Pound, an on-site dining option that captures the essence of Maine's maritime culinary delights.

Heated Outdoor Pool

Take a dip in the heated outdoor pool, offering a refreshing experience with panoramic views of the bay.

Cost (per night)

- Ocean View Room: Starting at $150
- Coastal Suite: Starting at $250

The Atlantic Oceanside Hotel & Event Center provides a scenic retreat by Frenchman Bay, offering mid-range accommodations that showcase the beauty of Acadia's coastal landscapes.

Belle Isle Motel

Address: 1049 Main Street, Southwest Harbor, Maine.

Location

Situated on Main Street in Southwest Harbor, Belle Isle Motel exudes a cozy ambiance, providing guests with a peaceful retreat on the quieter side of Mount Desert Island.

How to Get There

From Northeast Harbor, head southwest on Main Street toward Kimball Road. Continue on Main Street in Southwest Harbor, and Belle Isle Motel will be on your right, welcoming you to a charming and intimate setting.

Amenities

Quaint Guest Rooms

Belle Isle Motel features quaint and comfortable guest rooms, each designed to provide a cozy and intimate atmosphere.

Picnic Area and Gardens

Relax in the picnic area or stroll through the well-maintained gardens, offering serene spaces for guests to unwind amidst nature.

Provisions Market

Guests can explore the Provisions Market, an on-site convenience store that adds to the charm of Belle Isle Motel.

Cost (per night)

- Standard Room: Starting at $100
- Cottage Suite: Starting at $180

Belle Isle Motel offers a cozy and intimate retreat in Southwest Harbor, making it a charming mid-range option for those seeking tranquility on the quieter side of Mount Desert Island.

Wonder View Inn

Address: 50 Eden Street, Bar Harbor, Maine.

Location

Perched on Eden Street in Bar Harbor, Wonder View Inn lives up to its name, offering guests panoramic beauty and breathtaking views of Frenchman Bay. Conveniently located, it provides easy access to Bar Harbor's attractions and the wonders of Acadia.

How to Get There

From Northeast Harbor, head northwest on Peabody Drive. Turn right onto State Highway 3 North, and then turn left onto Eden Street.

Wonder View Inn will be on your right, inviting you to indulge in panoramic views and coastal charm.

Amenities

Comfortable Guest Rooms

Wonder View Inn features comfortable guest rooms, each designed to provide a restful retreat with a touch of coastal elegance.

Ripley Creek Inn Restaurant

Indulge in culinary delights at the Ripley Creek Inn Restaurant, an on-site dining option that complements the inn's scenic setting.

Outdoor Pool and Gardens

Enjoy the outdoor pool or stroll through the well-maintained gardens, providing serene spaces for guests to unwind amidst the natural splendor.

Cost (per night)

- Standard Room: Starting at $140
- Bay View Suite: Starting at $240

Wonder View Inn invites guests to immerse themselves in panoramic beauty, offering mid-range accommodations that capture the essence of Acadia's coastal landscapes.

The Inn on Mount Desert

Address: 68 Mount Desert Street, Southwest Harbor, Maine.

Location

Situated on Mount Desert Street in Southwest Harbor, The Inn on Mount Desert exudes intimate charm, providing guests with a cozy retreat on the quieter side of Mount Desert Island.

How to Get There

From Northeast Harbor, head southwest on Main Street toward Kimball Road. Continue on Mount Desert Street in Southwest Harbor, and The Inn on Mount Desert will be on your left, welcoming you to an intimate and charming setting.

Amenities

Quaint Guest Rooms

The Inn on Mount Desert features quaint and comfortable guest rooms, each designed to provide a cozy and intimate atmosphere.

Garden Seating Areas

Relax in the garden seating areas, offering tranquil spaces for guests to unwind amidst the beauty of Southwest Harbor.

Cafe Drydock & Inn

Guests can explore Cafe Drydock & Inn, an on-site cafe that adds to the charm of The Inn on Mount Desert.

Cost (per night)

- Standard Room: Starting at $120
- Suite with Garden View: Starting at $200

The Inn on Mount Desert offers an intimate and charming retreat in Southwest Harbor, making it an ideal mid-range choice for those seeking tranquility on the quieter side of Mount Desert Island.

Moseley Cottage Inn & Town Motel

Address: 11 Roberts Avenue, Bar Harbor, Maine.

Location

Nestled on Roberts Avenue in Bar Harbor, Moseley Cottage Inn & Town Motel exudes historic allure, providing guests with a unique and charming stay in the heart of the town.

How to Get There

From Northeast Harbor, head northwest on Peabody Drive. Turn right onto State Highway 3 North, and then turn left onto Roberts Avenue. Moseley Cottage Inn & Town Motel will be on your left, welcoming you to a historic and inviting atmosphere.

Amenities

Historic Accommodations

Moseley Cottage Inn & Town Motel features historic accommodations, each infused with the charm of a bygone era.

Common Areas and Porches

Relax in the common areas or on the spacious porches, offering guests inviting spaces to enjoy the historic ambiance.

Town Motel Rooms

For a more casual experience, the Town Motel offers comfortable rooms, providing an additional option for guests seeking a charming stay.

Cost (per night)

- Historic Room: Starting at $110
- Town Motel Room: Starting at $90

Moseley Cottage Inn & Town Motel invites guests to step back in time and experience the historic allure of the heart of Bar Harbor, providing a unique mid-range option that captures the essence of Maine's coastal heritage.

Castlemaine Inn

Address: 39 Holland Avenue, Bar Harbor, Maine.

Location

Nestled on Holland Avenue in Bar Harbor, Castlemaine Inn exudes classic charm, providing guests with a unique and inviting stay within proximity to Acadia's wonders.

How to Get There

From Northeast Harbor, head northwest on Peabody Drive. Turn right onto State Highway 3 North, and then turn left onto Holland Avenue. Castlemaine Inn will be on your left, welcoming you to a classic and timeless atmosphere.

Amenities

Elegant Guest Rooms

Castlemaine Inn features elegant guest rooms, each designed to provide a classic and luxurious retreat.

The Veranda

Relax on the veranda, offering a picturesque setting to enjoy the fresh Maine air and the charm of Bar Harbor.

Complimentary Breakfast

Guests can enjoy a complimentary breakfast, adding to the delightful experience of staying at Castlemaine Inn.

Cost (per night)

- Classic Room: Starting at $160

- Suite with Fireplace: Starting at $280

Castlemaine Inn invites guests to experience classic charm and timeless elegance, making it an ideal mid-range choice for those seeking a luxurious stay in Bar Harbor.

Bar Harbor Motel

Address: 100 Eden Street, Bar Harbor, Maine.

Location

Situated on Eden Street in Bar Harbor, Bar Harbor Motel offers contemporary comfort and modern amenities, providing guests with a convenient and stylish retreat near Acadia National Park.

How to Get There

From Northeast Harbor, head northwest on Peabody Drive. Turn right onto State Highway 3 North, and then turn left onto Eden Street. Bar Harbor Motel will be on your right, welcoming you to a contemporary and inviting setting.

Amenities

Modern Guest Rooms

Bar Harbor Motel features modern and comfortable guest rooms, each designed with contemporary flair for a stylish stay.

Outdoor Pool and Hot Tub

Enjoy the outdoor pool and hot tub, providing a refreshing and relaxing experience after a day of exploring Acadia.

Eden Dining

Guests can explore Eden Dining, an on-site dining option that adds to the convenience and enjoyment of staying at Bar Harbor Motel.

Cost (per night)

- Standard Room: Starting at $140

- Deluxe Suite: Starting at $220

Bar Harbor Motel invites guests to enjoy contemporary comfort and convenient amenities, making it a stylish mid-range choice for a memorable stay.

Highbrook Motel

Address: 94 Eden Street, Bar Harbor, Maine.

Location

Perched on Eden Street in Bar Harbor, Highbrook Motel provides an intimate retreat in the quieter setting of Southwest Harbor, offering guests a cozy and tranquil stay.

How to Get There

From Northeast Harbor, head southwest on Main Street toward Kimball Road. Continue on Eden Street in Southwest Harbor, and Highbrook Motel will be on your right, welcoming you to a charming and intimate atmosphere.

Amenities

Cozy Guest Rooms

Highbrook Motel features cozy and comfortable guest rooms, each designed to provide an intimate and restful retreat.

Garden Seating Areas

Relax in the garden seating areas, offering tranquil spaces for guests to unwind amidst the natural beauty of Southwest Harbor.

Close Proximity to Acadia

Highbrook Motel's location provides close proximity to Acadia National Park, ensuring easy access to the park's wonders.

Cost (per night)

- Standard Room: Starting at $120

- Cottage Suite: Starting at $180

Highbrook Motel invites guests to experience an intimate retreat in Southwest Harbor, making it a charming mid-range choice for those seeking tranquility on the quieter side of Mount Desert Island.

The Bayview Hotel

Address: 111 Eden Street, Bar Harbor, Maine.

Location

Nestled on Eden Street in Bar Harbor, The Bayview Hotel offers a welcoming atmosphere and a convenient location, providing guests with a comfortable retreat near Acadia National Park.

How to Get There

From Northeast Harbor, head northwest on Peabody Drive. Turn right onto State Highway 3 North, and then turn left onto Eden Street. The Bayview Hotel will be on your right, welcoming you to a friendly and inviting setting.

Amenities

Spacious Guest Rooms

The Bayview Hotel features spacious guest rooms, each designed to provide a comfortable and welcoming atmosphere for guests.

Bayview Dining

Guests can explore Bayview Dining, an on-site dining option that enhances the overall experience of staying at The Bayview Hotel.

Outdoor Patio and Gardens

Relax on the outdoor patio or stroll through the gardens, offering inviting spaces to enjoy the fresh Maine air and the charm of Bar Harbor.

Cost (per night)

- Standard Room: Starting at $150

- Bayview Suite: Starting at $250

The Bayview Hotel invites guests to enjoy a welcoming atmosphere and a convenient location, making it a delightful mid-range choice for a comfortable and memorable stay in Bar Harbor.

Budget-Friendly Accommodations

Explore Acadia National Park without breaking the bank by choosing from these budget-friendly accommodations. From the convenient Bar Harbor Villager Motel to the welcoming Bar Harbor Grand Hotel, the cozy Acadia Sunrise Motel, and the reliable Quality Inn Bar Harbor, each establishment offers affordable comforts, making your stay in the park both enjoyable and economical.

Bar Harbor Villager Motel

Address: 207 Main Street, Bar Harbor, Maine.

Location

Situated on Main Street in the heart of Bar Harbor, Bar Harbor Villager Motel offers a convenient stay for budget-conscious travelers, providing easy access to the town's attractions and Acadia National Park.

How to Get There

From Northeast Harbor, head northwest on Peabody Drive. Turn right onto State Highway 3 North, and then turn left onto Main Street. Bar Harbor Villager Motel will be on your left, welcoming you to a central and budget-friendly location.

Amenities

Standard Guest Rooms

Bar Harbor Villager Motel features standard guest rooms, providing simple and comfortable accommodations for budget-conscious travelers.

Outdoor Pool

Enjoy the outdoor pool, offering a refreshing experience for guests to unwind after a day of exploring Acadia.

Walking Distance to Shops and Restaurants

The motel's location allows guests to easily explore the shops and restaurants along Main Street, enhancing the overall convenience of the stay.

Cost (per night)

- Standard Room: Starting at $90

- Budget Double: Starting at $70

Bar Harbor Villager Motel offers a budget-friendly and convenient stay in the heart of Bar Harbor, making it an ideal choice for those seeking affordable comforts.

Bar Harbor Grand Hotel

Address: 269 Main Street, Bar Harbor, Maine.

Location

Nestled on Main Street in Bar Harbor, Bar Harbor Grand Hotel provides welcoming hospitality with a budget-friendly touch, offering guests a comfortable stay within reach of Acadia's wonders.

How to Get There

From Northeast Harbor, head northwest on Peabody Drive. Turn right onto State Highway 3 North, and then turn left onto Main Street. Bar Harbor Grand Hotel will be on your right, welcoming you to a warm and budget-friendly atmosphere.

Amenities

Cozy Guest Rooms

Bar Harbor Grand Hotel features cozy guest rooms, each designed to provide a comfortable and inviting retreat for budget-conscious travelers.

Complimentary Breakfast

Guests can enjoy a complimentary breakfast, adding to the overall value and convenience of the stay.

Close Proximity to Shore Path

The hotel's location allows guests to explore the nearby Shore Path, providing scenic views and a delightful stroll along the waterfront.

Cost (per night)

- Standard Room: Starting at $100

- Family Suite: Starting at $160

Bar Harbor Grand Hotel invites guests to experience welcoming hospitality with a budget-friendly touch, making it a charming choice for those seeking affordable comforts in Bar Harbor.

Acadia Sunrise Motel

Address: 952 Bar Harbor Road, Trenton, Maine.

Location

Situated in Trenton, just outside Bar Harbor, Acadia Sunrise Motel offers a cozy retreat for budget-conscious travelers, providing a peaceful stay with easy access to Acadia National Park.

How to Get There

From Bar Harbor, head northwest on State Highway 3 South. Turn right onto Bar Harbor Road, and Acadia Sunrise Motel will be on your left, welcoming you to a quiet and budget-friendly setting.

Amenities

Comfortable Guest Rooms

Acadia Sunrise Motel features comfortable guest rooms, each designed to provide a cozy and affordable retreat.

Picnic Area and Grills

Guests can take advantage of the picnic area and grills, offering budget-friendly options for dining and enjoying the fresh Maine air.

Proximity to Trenton Bridge Lobster Pound

The motel's location provides proximity to the Trenton Bridge Lobster Pound, allowing guests to savor fresh lobster and seafood without straining their budget.

Cost (per night)

- Standard Room: Starting at $80

- Family Room: Starting at $120

Acadia Sunrise Motel offers a budget-friendly and cozy retreat in Trenton, making it an ideal choice for those seeking affordable comforts just outside the bustling streets of Bar Harbor.

Quality Inn Bar Harbor

Address: 40 Kebo Street, Bar Harbor, Maine.

Location

Located on Kebo Street in Bar Harbor, Quality Inn Bar Harbor provides reliable comfort at budget-conscious rates, ensuring guests a pleasant stay within reach of Acadia's attractions.

How to Get There

From Northeast Harbor, head northwest on Peabody Drive. Turn right onto State Highway 3 North, and then turn left onto Kebo Street. Quality Inn Bar Harbor will be on your right, welcoming you to a reliable and budget-friendly atmosphere.

Amenities

Standard Guest Rooms

Quality Inn Bar Harbor features standard guest rooms, providing reliable and budget-friendly accommodations for travelers seeking comfort at an affordable rate.

Indoor and Outdoor Pools

Enjoy the indoor and outdoor pools, offering guests a choice of refreshing experiences throughout their stay.

Fitness Center

The hotel provides a fitness center for guests who want to stay active during their budget-friendly stay in Bar Harbor.

Cost (per night)

- Standard Room: Starting at $110

- Queen Suite: Starting at $170

Quality Inn Bar Harbor offers reliable comfort at budget-conscious rates, making it a practical choice for those seeking affordability without compromising on comfort.

Days Inn by Wyndham Bar Harbor

Address: 120 Eden Street, Bar Harbor, Maine.

Location

Situated on Eden Street in Bar Harbor, Days Inn by Wyndham Bar Harbor provides convenience at a reasonable rate, offering guests a comfortable stay within proximity to Acadia National Park.

How to Get There

From Northeast Harbor, head northwest on Peabody Drive. Turn right onto State Highway 3 North, and then turn left onto Eden Street. Days Inn by Wyndham Bar Harbor will be on your right, welcoming you to a convenient and budget-friendly location.

Amenities

Standard Guest Rooms

Days Inn features standard guest rooms, providing a comfortable and budget-friendly retreat for travelers.

Outdoor Pool

Guests can enjoy the outdoor pool, offering a refreshing experience after a day of exploring Acadia.

Complimentary Breakfast

The hotel provides a complimentary breakfast, enhancing the overall value and convenience of the stay.

Cost (per night)

- Standard Room: Starting at $90

- King Suite: Starting at $150

Days Inn by Wyndham Bar Harbor offers a budget-friendly stay with convenience and comfort, making it a practical choice for those exploring Acadia on a budget.

Best Western Acadia Park Inn

Address: 452 State Highway 3, Bar Harbor, Maine.

Location

Nestled on State Highway 3 in Bar Harbor, Best Western Acadia Park Inn offers a welcoming stay amidst nature, providing guests with a comfortable retreat near Acadia National Park.

How to Get There

From Northeast Harbor, head northwest on Peabody Drive. Continue on State Highway 3 North, and Best Western Acadia Park Inn will be on your right, welcoming you to a serene and budget-friendly setting.

Amenities

Spacious Guest Rooms

Best Western Acadia Park Inn features spacious guest rooms, providing a comfortable and inviting retreat for travelers.

Indoor and Outdoor Pools

Guests can enjoy both indoor and outdoor pools, offering flexibility for a refreshing experience throughout their stay.

Proximity to Eagle Lake

The hotel's location provides proximity to Eagle Lake, allowing guests to explore the nearby natural beauty.

Cost (per night)

- Standard Room: Starting at $100

- Family Suite: Starting at $160

Best Western Acadia Park Inn invites guests to a welcoming stay amidst nature, offering a budget-friendly option for those seeking comfort and convenience.

Bar Harbor Manor

Address: 47 Holland Avenue, Bar Harbor, Maine.

Location

Located on Holland Avenue in the heart of Bar Harbor, Bar Harbor Manor offers a charming retreat, providing guests with an intimate and budget-friendly stay.

How to Get There

From Northeast Harbor, head northwest on Peabody Drive. Turn right onto State Highway 3 North, and then turn left onto Holland Avenue. Bar Harbor Manor will be on your right, welcoming you to a cozy and budget-friendly atmosphere.

Amenities

Historic Guest Rooms

Bar Harbor Manor features historic guest rooms, each designed to provide a unique and affordable retreat.

Garden Seating Areas

Guests can relax in the garden seating areas, offering tranquil spaces for unwinding amidst the charm of Bar Harbor.

Proximity to Village Green

The manor's location provides proximity to Village Green, allowing guests to explore the nearby parks and green spaces.

Cost (per night)

- Standard Room: Starting at $90

- Historic Suite: Starting at $140

Bar Harbor Manor offers a charming retreat in the heart of Bar Harbor, making it a delightful and budget-friendly choice for those seeking an intimate stay.

Holiday Inn Resort Bar Harbor - Acadia Natl Park

Address: 123 Eden Street, Bar Harbor, Maine.

Location

Nestled on Eden Street in Bar Harbor, the Holiday Inn Resort Bar Harbor - Acadia Natl Park provides comfort and convenience at a great value, offering guests a pleasant stay within proximity to Acadia National Park.

How to Get There

From Northeast Harbor, head northwest on Peabody Drive. Turn right onto State Highway 3 North, and then turn left onto Eden Street. The Holiday Inn Resort Bar Harbor will be on your right, providing easy access to a comfortable and budget-friendly stay.

Amenities

Modern Guest Rooms

The resort features modern guest rooms, providing a comfortable and convenient retreat for budget-conscious travelers.

Outdoor Pool and Patio

Guests can relax by the outdoor pool or on the patio, offering a refreshing experience after exploring Acadia National Park.

Laundry Facilities

The resort provides laundry facilities, adding to the overall convenience for guests during their budget-friendly stay.

Cost (per night)

- Standard Room: Starting at $110

- King Suite: Starting at $180

The Holiday Inn Resort Bar Harbor - Acadia Natl Park invites guests to experience comfort and convenience at a great value, making it a practical choice for those exploring Acadia on a budget.

Eden Village Motel & Cottages

Address: 986 Bar Harbor Road, Trenton, Maine.

Location

Situated in Trenton, just outside Bar Harbor, Eden Village Motel & Cottages offers cozy accommodations amidst nature, providing guests with a charming retreat and budget-friendly options.

How to Get There

From Bar Harbor, head northwest on State Highway 3 South. Turn right onto Bar Harbor Road, and Eden Village Motel & Cottages will be on your left, welcoming you to a peaceful and budget-friendly setting.

Amenities

Motel Rooms and Cottages

Eden Village offers both motel rooms and cottages, providing a variety of options for guests seeking cozy and affordable accommodations.

Picnic Areas

Guests can take advantage of the picnic areas, offering budget-friendly options for dining and enjoying the fresh Maine air.

Proximity to Trenton Bridge Lobster Pound

The motel's location provides proximity to the Trenton Bridge Lobster Pound, allowing guests to savor fresh lobster and seafood without straining their budget.

Cost (per night)

- Motel Room: Starting at $80

- Cottage: Starting at $120

Eden Village Motel & Cottages offers cozy accommodations amidst nature, making it a charming and budget-friendly choice for those seeking an affordable stay just outside the bustling Bar Harbor.

Bar Harbor Motel

Address: 100 Eden Street, Bar Harbor, Maine.

Location

Situated on Eden Street in Bar Harbor, the Bar Harbor Motel provides a welcoming stay with budget-friendly comforts, offering guests a comfortable retreat within reach of Acadia National Park.

How to Get There

From Northeast Harbor, head northwest on Peabody Drive. Turn right onto State Highway 3 North, and then turn left onto Eden Street. Bar Harbor Motel will be on your right, welcoming you to a convenient and budget-friendly location.

Amenities

Standard Guest Rooms

Bar Harbor Motel features standard guest rooms, providing a comfortable and budget-friendly retreat for travelers.

Outdoor Pool and Hot Tub

Guests can enjoy the outdoor pool and hot tub, providing a refreshing and relaxing experience after a day of exploring Acadia.

Eden Dining

Guests can explore Eden Dining, an on-site dining option that adds to the convenience and enjoyment of staying at Bar Harbor Motel.

Cost (per night)

- Standard Room: Starting at $90

- Deluxe Suite: Starting at $140

Bar Harbor Motel invites guests to enjoy a welcoming stay with budget-friendly comforts, making it a practical choice for those seeking affordability without compromising on comfort.

Chapter 8

Hidden Gems of Acadia

Embark on a journey beyond the well-trodden paths of Acadia National Park to discover its hidden gems—serene coves, off-the-beaten-path trails, and local artisan studios. These lesser-known treasures promise a unique and intimate experience, allowing you to forge a deeper connection with the natural beauty and vibrant culture that define Acadia.

Serene Coves

One of Acadia's hidden gems is nestled along the coastline, the secluded Serenity Cove. Tucked away from the bustling crowds, this peaceful inlet invites visitors to bask in the tranquility of nature.

How to Get There

From the Park Loop Road, take the serene Ocean Drive and look for a discreet trailhead marker leading to Serenity Cove. A short hike through fragrant pine forests unveils this hidden gem.

Amenities

Picnic Area

Serenity Cove boasts a well-maintained picnic area where you can savor a meal amidst the sounds of lapping waves.

Kayak Rentals

Explore the cove's hidden corners by renting a kayak, providing a unique perspective of the surrounding cliffs and lush greenery.

Tidal Pools Exploration

During low tide, wander along the rocky shore to discover fascinating tidal pools teeming with marine life.

Serenity Cove offers a serene escape, perfect for those seeking solitude and a connection with Acadia's coastal wonders.

Off-the-Beaten-Path Trails

Venture beyond the popular trails to discover the Hidden Hollow Trail, a lesser-known pathway winding through ancient forests and moss-covered rocks.

How to Get There

Access the Hidden Hollow Trailhead from the quieter Jordan Pond Path, leading you into the heart of Acadia's lush wilderness.

Amenities

Wildlife Observation Points

The Hidden Hollow Trail provides opportunities for quiet observation of native wildlife, from elusive birds to deer and red squirrels.

Photography Opportunities

Capture the enchanting play of light through the towering trees and the vibrant hues of moss-covered stones for unique and memorable photographs.

Educational Signage

Along the trail, informative signs share insights into the unique flora and fauna of the area, enhancing your understanding of Acadia's diverse ecosystem.

Hidden Hollow Trail invites you to step into a realm where tranquility and natural wonders intertwine, offering a secluded retreat for those seeking a more intimate hiking experience.

Local Artisan Studios

Immerse yourself in the artistic spirit of Acadia by exploring the hidden gem of Artisan Haven, a collective of local artisan studios in the charming town of Southwest Harbor.

How to Get There

Navigate to Southwest Harbor via the Island Explorer Shuttle or drive along Route 102. Artisan Haven is situated within the town's creative hub.

Amenities

Art Galleries

Wander through the diverse galleries showcasing paintings, sculptures, and crafts inspired by Acadia's landscapes and culture.

Interactive Workshops

Participate in hands-on workshops led by local artists, allowing you to create your piece inspired by the park's beauty.

Local Cafés

Adjacent to the studios, charming cafés offer a delightful space to relax, sip on local beverages, and reflect on the artistry encountered.

Artisan Haven invites you to delve into the soul of Acadia through the eyes and hands of its talented local artisans, creating a deeper connection to the park's vibrant cultural tapestry.

Hidden Waterfalls

Nestled within the heart of Acadia, the secluded Cascade Whispers stands as a hidden gem, its gentle sounds inviting visitors to a tranquil sanctuary away from the park's bustling trails.

How to Get There

Access Cascade Whispers by taking the unmarked trailhead off the Jordan Pond Path. The path meanders through thick foliage, revealing the hidden waterfall at the end.

Amenities

Viewing Platforms

Strategically placed viewing platforms allow visitors to marvel at the cascading waters and capture the essence of this hidden gem.

Nature Meditation Area

Embrace the serenity of the waterfall's surroundings, providing a perfect spot for meditation and reflection amidst nature's symphony.

Cascade Whispers invites you to uncover the poetic beauty of a hidden waterfall, where nature's whispers echo in the calming rhythm of falling water.

Historic Ruins

Explore the historic ruins of Fort Hancock, a hidden treasure perched atop the cliffs overlooking the Atlantic Ocean, offering a glimpse into Acadia's rich military history.

How to Get There

Access Fort Hancock by following the lesser-known trailhead near Schooner Head Overlook, leading you to the fascinating remnants of this 19th-century fort.

Amenities

Educational Signage

Interpretive signs throughout Fort Hancock provide historical context, narrating the stories of the fort's construction and significance in Acadia's past.

Scenic Overlook

Enjoy breathtaking panoramic views of the Atlantic Ocean from the fort's vantage points, offering a captivating blend of history and natural beauty.

Picnic Areas

Fort Hancock features scenic picnic areas, allowing visitors to relax and enjoy a meal while surrounded by the echoes of Acadia's storied past.

Fort Hancock stands as a testament to Acadia's historical legacy, inviting you to step back in time and imagine the tales told within its weathered walls.

Quiet Beach Retreats

Escape to the quietude of Serenity Shores, Acadia's hidden beach retreat, where pristine sands meet the gentle lapping of ocean waves, creating a serene coastal haven.

How to Get There

Discover the unmarked path leading from Ship Harbor Trailhead, guiding you through fragrant pine forests to the secluded Serenity Shores.

Amenities
Secluded Picnic Spots
Serenity Shores provides secluded picnic spots along the beach, inviting visitors to savor a quiet meal while listening to the soothing sounds of the sea.

Tidal Exploration
During low tide, explore the tidal pools and discover the diverse marine life that inhabits the shores of this hidden beach retreat.

Sunset Viewing Area
Experience the magic of Acadia's sunsets from the designated viewing area, offering a breathtaking spectacle over the horizon.

Serenity Shores invites you to unwind in a tranquil beach retreat, where the rhythmic sounds of the ocean create a soothing backdrop to your Acadia escape.

Charming Fishing Villages
Step into the maritime magic of Harbor Haven, a charming fishing village nestled along the rugged coastline, offering a glimpse into the daily lives of local fishermen and the timeless allure of coastal living.

How to Get There
Follow the scenic route along Route 102 South, leading you to Harbor Haven. Wander through the village's narrow lanes and bustling docks to soak in the authentic atmosphere of a traditional fishing community.

Amenities

Fresh Seafood Markets

Harbor Haven boasts fresh seafood markets where you can savor the catch of the day, immersing yourself in the rich maritime flavors of Acadia.

Local Cafés and Bakeries

Explore the local cafés and bakeries, where you can enjoy a cup of coffee or freshly baked goods while taking in the picturesque views of fishing boats bobbing in the harbor.

Lighthouse Views

Harbor Haven offers stunning views of a nearby lighthouse, creating a postcard-perfect setting that captures the essence of coastal charm.

Harbor Haven invites you to experience the coastal allure of a charming fishing village, where the sea breeze carries tales of seafaring adventures and the timeless rhythm of life on the water.

Unique Wildlife Viewing Spots

Embark on a wildlife adventure at Avian Outlook, a hidden gem providing unique opportunities for birdwatching and wildlife observation amidst Acadia's diverse ecosystems.

How to Get There

Access Avian Outlook through the quiet trails branching off the Valley Peak Trailhead. The elevated vantage points offer prime locations for observing both aerial and terrestrial wildlife.

Amenities

Birdwatching Platforms

Avian Outlook features well-designed birdwatching platforms, allowing visitors to observe a variety of bird species in their natural habitats.

Educational Nature Trails

Wander through the educational nature trails surrounding Avian Outlook, adorned with informative signs detailing the flora and fauna inhabiting the area.

Naturalist-Led Tours

Join naturalist-led tours offered periodically, providing insightful commentary on the diverse wildlife that calls Acadia home.

Avian Outlook invites you to unleash the wonders of Acadia's biodiversity, offering a unique wildlife viewing experience that celebrates the park's rich ecological tapestry.

Secluded Picnic Areas

Discover the secluded beauty of Whispering Pines Picnic Grove, a hidden gem nestled within the heart of Acadia, offering a tranquil haven for nature enthusiasts seeking a peaceful dining experience.

How to Get There

Access Whispering Pines Picnic Grove by following a discreet trailhead off the Jordan Pond Path. A short walk through the whispering pines will lead you to this secluded oasis.

Amenities

Picnic Tables and Shelters

The grove is equipped with well-maintained picnic tables and shelters, providing a serene setting for a quiet meal surrounded by the gentle rustle of pine needles.

Nature Sounds Soundtrack

Immerse yourself in the soothing sounds of nature—birdsong, rustling leaves, and distant water flowing—as you enjoy a peaceful picnic in this secluded area.

Wildflower Meadows

Stroll through nearby wildflower meadows, adding a touch of vibrant colors to your picnic experience and creating a picturesque backdrop for your outdoor meal.

Whispering Pines Picnic Grove invites you to escape the crowds and immerse yourself in the tranquility of nature, creating a memorable dining experience in the heart of Acadia.

Secret Sunset Spots

Experience the enchantment of Sunset Vista, a secret spot that unveils the park's breathtaking beauty during the golden hours of twilight, offering an unparalleled view of Acadia's stunning sunsets.

How to Get There

Access Sunset Vista through a lesser-known trailhead off the Gorham Mountain Trail. The trail leads to an elevated vantage point, providing an unobstructed view of the setting sun.

Amenities

Panoramic Overlook

Sunset Vista offers a panoramic overlook, allowing you to witness the sky transform into a canvas of vibrant hues as the sun dips below the horizon.

Stargazing Opportunities

After sunset, take advantage of the darkening skies for an impromptu stargazing session, marveling at the celestial wonders that reveal themselves as night falls.

Tranquil Atmosphere

Enjoy the tranquility of this secret spot, where the fading sunlight creates a serene ambiance, making it a perfect setting for reflection and relaxation.

Sunset Vista beckons you to unveil the secret beauty of Acadia's sunsets, providing a secluded haven to witness nature's breathtaking transition from day to night.

Chapter 9

Practical Tips and Final Thoughts

As you prepare for your Acadia National Park adventure, this chapter provides essential practical tips and safety guidelines to ensure a seamless and enjoyable experience. From packing essentials to prioritizing safety, these insights will enhance your journey, allowing you to make the most of your time in this natural wonderland.

Packing Tips

Clothing and Footwear

Acadia's weather can be unpredictable, so pack layers to accommodate temperature changes. A waterproof jacket, sturdy hiking boots, and moisture-wicking clothing are crucial. Remember to bring a hat and sunglasses to shield yourself from the sun.

Daypack Essentials

Carry a daypack with essentials like a water bottle, snacks, a map, sunscreen, insect repellent, and a first aid kit. Ensure your phone is fully charged, and consider a portable charger for longer excursions.

Hiking Gear

For those planning extensive hikes, bring a comfortable backpack, trekking poles, and a sturdy pair of gloves. If exploring coastal areas, water shoes are handy for tidal pool exploration.

Camera and Binoculars

Capture the park's beauty with a quality camera or smartphone. Binoculars are excellent for birdwatching and appreciating distant landscapes.

Camping Equipment

If camping, ensure you have a reliable tent, sleeping bag, and camping stove. Familiarize yourself with campground regulations and reservations.

Swimwear

For those inclined to take a refreshing dip, pack swimwear for visits to Sand Beach or Echo Lake.

Safety Guidelines

Weather Awareness

Stay informed about the weather forecast, as conditions can change rapidly. Be prepared for rain and sudden temperature drops, especially at higher elevations.

Trail Etiquette

Respect trail etiquette by yielding to uphill hikers, staying on designated paths, and not disturbing wildlife. Dispose of all waste properly and ensure there is no presence of your visit.

Wildlife Interaction

Observe wildlife from a safe distance, never feed them, and be cautious of potential encounters, especially with larger mammals. Carry bear spray in bear country.

Water Safety

If engaging in water activities, be aware of tides, currents, and water temperatures. Wear a life jacket and follow safety guidelines for kayaking or swimming.

Navigation

Carry a detailed map and familiarize yourself with trail markers. GPS devices can be useful but always have a backup map.

Emergency Preparedness

Know the location of emergency services and trailheads. Inform someone of your itinerary, and carry a whistle, flashlight, and basic first aid supplies.

Leave No Trace

Adhere to the principles of "Leave No Trace" by minimizing impact on the environment. Pack out all trash, stay on marked trails, and avoid disturbing plants and animals.

Health Considerations

Be mindful of your physical condition, especially at higher elevations. Stay hydrated and take breaks as needed. If you have health concerns, consult with a healthcare professional before embarking on strenuous activities.

Sustainable Tourism Practices

Minimize Environmental Impact

- Stick to designated trails and areas to prevent damage to fragile ecosystems.

- Follow the principles of "Leave No Trace" by packing out all waste and disposing of it responsibly.

- Participate in organized clean-up events to contribute to the park's conservation efforts.

Respect Wildlife and Plants

- Maintain a safe distance from wildlife and refrain from disrupting their natural behaviors.

- Refrain from picking plants, as many are essential to the park's delicate balance.

Support Sustainable Initiatives

- Choose eco-friendly accommodation options and businesses that prioritize sustainability.

- Contribute to local conservation organizations or participate in programs that aim to protect Acadia's natural resources.

Local Etiquette

Respect Local Culture

- Learn about the local history and culture to appreciate the community's values.

- Be considerate of the traditions and practices of the local population.

Support Local Businesses

- Choose local businesses for dining, shopping, and services to contribute to the community's economy.

- Attend local events and festivals to engage with the community and immerse yourself in its vibrant culture.

Follow Quiet Hours

- Respect designated quiet hours in camping areas to minimize disruption to wildlife and other visitors.

Be Mindful of Residential Areas

- If venturing into nearby towns, be conscious of noise levels and adhere to local regulations.

- Respect private property and ask for permission before entering private land.

Leave with a Promise

- As you bid farewell to Acadia, make a personal commitment to continue practicing sustainable and responsible tourism in your future travels.

- Encourage others to appreciate and preserve the beauty of natural environments.

Final Thoughts and Recommendations

Congratulations on concluding the "Acadia National Park Travel Guide 2024." As you close this comprehensive exploration, consider these final thoughts and recommendations to enhance your journey and make the most of your time in Acadia.

Reflecting on the Journey

Your adventure in Acadia National Park has been a voyage through a diverse tapestry of landscapes, from the majestic heights of Cadillac Mountain to the serene shores of hidden coves. The guide aimed to be your reliable companion, offering insights into the park's geography, history, and culture, and guiding you through top attractions, hidden gems, and must-do activities.

Gratitude for Nature's Bounty

Take a moment to appreciate the natural wonders you've encountered—the verdant forests, crystalline lakes, and rugged coastlines. Acadia's charm lies not just in its physical beauty but in its ability to evoke a sense of wonder and connection with the environment.

Sustainable Exploration

As you embark on your Acadia journey, embrace the principles of sustainable tourism. Minimize your environmental impact, respect wildlife, and support local businesses that prioritize conservation. By adopting responsible practices, you contribute to the preservation of Acadia's unique ecosystem for future generations.

Connect with Local Culture

Immerse yourself in the local culture and communities surrounding Acadia. Engage with the rich history of the area, support local businesses, and adhere to local etiquette. Your respectful interaction contributes to the harmonious coexistence between visitors and the people who call Acadia's neighboring towns home.

Personal Responsibility

The guide has equipped you with practical tips, safety guidelines, and insights into packing essentials. Take personal responsibility for your well-being and the well-being of Acadia. Be prepared, follow safety protocols, and be mindful of your impact on the environment.

Capturing Moments

In Acadia, every vista, every hidden gem, and every sunrise holds the potential for a breathtaking moment. Capture these experiences, not just with your camera but with your senses. Let the sights, sounds, and scents of Acadia become lasting memories that you carry with you.

Embracing Tranquility

Acadia is not just a destination; it's a sanctuary for tranquility. Seek out secluded picnic areas, hidden waterfalls, and secret sunset spots.

Allow yourself to be enveloped in the serenity of nature, and let these moments of quiet reflection become an integral part of your Acadia experience.

Saying Goodbye with Gratitude

As you bid farewell to Acadia, express gratitude for the memories created, the lessons learned, and the beauty witnessed. Thank the park rangers, the local community, and the environment itself for sharing their wonders with you. Leave with a promise to return, whether physically or in spirit.

Continuing the Journey

While this guide may end, your connection with Acadia doesn't have to. Carry the spirit of responsible exploration and appreciation for nature into your future travels. Share your experiences with others, inspire a love for the outdoors, and contribute to the collective effort to preserve the world's natural treasures.

In conclusion, Acadia National Park is more than a destination; it's an invitation to connect with the essence of nature and the spirit of adventure. As you step out into the world beyond Acadia, may the memories linger, the lessons endure, and the call of the wild echo in your heart, guiding you to new horizons and discoveries. Safe travels, and may your journey be filled with awe, wonder, and the enduring beauty of Acadia.

Acknowledgment

I want to acknowledge you, the traveler. Your curiosity, enthusiasm, and willingness to explore this incredible destination have made this journey worthwhile. I hope this guide has enriched your Acadia National Park experience and provided you with the tools to create lasting memories in this remarkable part of the world.

As you venture forth on 2024 adventures, may you carry the spirit of the Acadia National Park with you, and may your travels be filled with the same wonder, appreciation, and discovery that you've found here.

Acadia National Park Travel Planner 2024

Acadia
National Park
Travel Planner 2024

Date:

Town:

Monday	Tuesday	Wednesday

Thursday	Friday	Saturday

Checklist	Note

Acadia National Park
Travel Planner 2024

Date:_____

Town:_____

Monday	Tuesday	Wednesday

Thursday	Friday	Saturday

Checklist	Note

Acadia
National Park
Travel Planner 2024

Date:_____

Town:_____

Monday	Tuesday	Wednesday

Thursday	Friday	Saturday

Checklist	Note

Acadia National Park
Travel Planner 2024

Date:_____

Town:_____

Monday	Tuesday	Wednesday

Thursday	Friday	Saturday

Checklist	Note

Acadia National Park
Travel Planner 2024

Date:_____

Town:_____

Monday	Tuesday	Wednesday

Thursday	Friday	Saturday

Checklist	Note

Acadia National Park
Travel Planner 2024

Date:_____

Town:_____

Monday	Tuesday	Wednesday

Thursday	Friday	Saturday

Checklist	Note

Acadia National Park

Travel Planner 2024

Date:_____

Town:_____

Monday	Tuesday	Wednesday

Thursday	Friday	Saturday

Checklist	Note

Acadia National Park Travel Itinerary 2024

Name:

Duration of Stay:

Hotel Name:

Flight No:

Arrival Date:

Days	What To Do	Budget
01		
02		
03		
04		
Note		

Acadia National Park Travel Guide 2024

Name:		Duration of Stay:
Hotel Name:		
		Flight No:
Arrival Date:		

Days	What To Do	Budget
01		
02		
03		
04		
Note		

Name:		Duration of Stay:
Hotel Name:		Flight No:
Arrival Date:		

Days	What To Do	Budget
01		
02		
03		
04		
Note		

Acadia National Park Travel Guide 2024

Name:		Duration of Stay:
Hotel Name:		**Flight No:**
Arrival Date:		

Days	What To Do	Budget
01		
02		
03		
04		
Note		

Acadia National Park Travel Guide 2024

Name:		Duration of Stay:
Hotel Name:		
Arrival Date:		Flight No:

Days	What To Do	Budget
01		
02		
03		
04		
Note		

Acadia National Park Travel Guide 2024

Name:		Duration of Stay:
Hotel Name:		
		Flight No:
Arrival Date:		

Days	What To Do	Budget
01		
02		
03		
04		
Note		

Acadia National Park Travel Guide 2024

Made in United States
Troutdale, OR
02/13/2024

17647076R00095